Self-Defense
for Women
THE WEST POINT WAY

Susan Goldner Peterson

Director of Women's Self-Defense,
Department of Physical Education,
United States Military Academy

SIMON AND SCHUSTER/NEW YORK

Designed by Judith Neuman
Manufactured in the United States of America
Printed by The Murray Printing Company
Bound by The Book Press, Inc.
1 2 3 4 5 6 7 8 9 10

Library of Congress Cataloging in Publication Data

Peterson, Susan Goldner.
    Self-defense for women.

    1.   Self-defense for women.   I.   Title.
GV1111.5.P47   613.6'6   78-12586

ISBN 0-671-23086-7

This book is dedicated to Peterson, my loving husband.

ACKNOWLEDGMENTS

*Many thanks to Cadets Laura Welsh and Tom Grace
for their patience and efforts as models for all the
photographs. I also express my appreciation to Cpt.
Monte Anderson and Sgt. Gene Garren (United States
Army) for their expertise, assistance and professional
guidance in helping to develop the self-defense
program for women at West Point. Finally, heartfelt
appreciation to my parents for all their support and
encouragement throughout the years.*

Photographs by: Robert W. Caudy, Horizon Photography

CONTENTS

PREFACE

The primary mission of the Department of Physical
Education of the United States Military Academy is
to train and develop every cadet so that upon gradua-
tion, each cadet possesses the physical ability necessary
to be an officer in the United States Army. An integral
part of that training is to require every cadet to partici-
pate in an extensive combative program. For the male
cadets, the core of the combative program is instruction
in boxing and wrestling, activities that involve both
offensive and defensive skills. For the women cadets,
the combative program is geared to develop in each
woman cadet the capacity to defend herself in a variety
of situations—military and nonmilitary alike.

Entitled Self-Defense I and Self-Defense II, the block
of combative instruction for women cadets has evolved
from considerable research and interaction with other
colleges and universities, the FBI, police departments,
martial arts experts, and the Military Police Branch of
the Army. This curriculum is the basis for *Self-Defense
for Women: The West Point Way*. It has been a

9

successful program for the women cadets and will
prove to be successful for you. Read and learn the
techniques presented in the book's fifteen chapters.
Your life may depend on it!

1 Survival

"Mom and Daughter Found Dead in Their Queens Home" • "Woman Stabbed to Death at Noon on Lincoln Center IRT Platform" (more than a dozen persons witnessed the murder) • " 'No One Is Safe' States South Side Chicago Neighborhood Council" • "85, She's Tied, Gagged and Slain" • "18-Year-Old Dropout Pleads Guilty in Rape Case" • "Husband, Wife Robbed by Youths" • "Husband Batters Wife and Kids"

The preceding newspaper headlines are a stark reminder that survival in the urban jungles of today's society is becoming an around-the-clock aspect of life for women of all ages. No woman is immune from the actions of the criminal elements of society. No locality is spared the violent rise in lawlessness.

Given the dramatic increase in the number of rapes, muggings and other violent crimes involving women, every woman is forced to assume a greater degree of responsibility for her own safety. A working knowledge

11

of the basic principles of personal self-defense can play an important role in this task.

• *Self-Defense for Women: The West Point Way* offers women of all ages an inclusive overview of practical and proven techniques of self-defense. A woman who has mastered many of the skills that will enable her to protect herself from bodily harm will be better prepared to react rationally and sensibly in a potentially dangerous situation. Such preparation could easily make the difference in a life-and-death confrontation.

Just as West Point has traditionally trained the finest in American youth to be soldier–leaders, the venerable institution on the Hudson has committed itself to offering its newly admitted female cadets the finest in self-defense instruction. This book is an overview of that block of instruction. From preteens to grandmothers, *Self-Defense for Women: The West Point Way* offers a common sense, step-by-step approach to self-defense for women everywhere.

The *Practical* Approach to Self-Defense

The most common sense advice that should be followed by all women is to avoid potentially dangerous situations if at all possible. While no locality or hour of the day is exempt from the actions of criminals, some situations (e.g., riding a lonely subway car, walking alone at night, hitchhiking, etc.) are obviously more dangerous than others. Preventing an assault from occurring is *always* the most appropriate course of action. A woman who runs away from, or who talks her way out of a potential assault, is obviously less vulnerable to injury than one who is forced to defend herself against an adversary who, in most instances, will be larger and stronger than she. Physical actions for self-defense purposes should be employed only when the victim cannot avoid the assault.

On the other hand, a woman should not be a passive victim who panics or completely succumbs to the demands of her assailant. Unless her actions would obviously result in a serious injury to herself, a woman should attempt to defend herself when assaulted. This defense may take a variety of forms. Many women have successfully remained calm and talked their way out of an attack situation. Talking may also momentarily distract the assailant so that other more direct types of defenses may be used.

Since most criminals do not expect a woman to defend herself, self-defense techniques can give any woman an important advantage—the element of surprise. In addition, an attacker who sees that he has to fight his victim may flee in hopes of finding an easier mark! Thus, it is important to respond to a dangerous situation quickly, skillfully, and with confidence.

One primary response to a dangerous situation is to have the victim shout for *HELP*. While there is some professional disagreement over the desirability of having a victim shout for assistance, most agencies recommend such an action. Shouting is a distraction that can easily startle the attacker and cause him to momentarily halt his assault. This pause may then permit the victim to use appropriate self-defense techniques to allow her to escape. In addition, shouting in a populated area may attract the assistance of other individuals. Even if outside help does not immediately arrive, the attacker may be scared away because of his fear of being caught. Several police departments in major U.S. cities have found that women who shout for help are more successful in getting assistance if they cry "FIRE" rather than "RAPE" or "HELP." Although some people may not want to get involved with someone else's individual problems, they may respond to the more general and less personal cry of "FIRE"!

Martial Arts Are Not the Complete Answer

As the lawlessness involving women has increased, the need for prudent measures to counteract the personal dangers has also increased. Women who are interested in becoming more prepared to handle potentially dangerous situations should understand that effective self-defense techniques are not genetically passed on from parent to offspring. They must be learned and then practiced. Physical practice (alone or with a partner), as well as mental practice, is required. This book presents a logical, detailed program for the physical practice of the basic self-defense skills. In addition, the individual should think about the basic self-defense techniques and should constantly review these procedures mentally (e.g., if walking alone at night, are you thinking what you would do if someone grabbed and started choking you from behind?).

Another major factor that should be considered by all women is that martial arts skills are not the complete answer for self-protection. As the interest in self-defense programs for women increases, many different forms of the Martial Arts have been advocated as the "best tool" for self-protection for women (e.g., judo, karate, aikido, Tae Kwan Do, etc.). It should be remembered, however, that these Martial Art techniques are usually highly complex. As such, these skills frequently require many hours of tedious practice to be perfected. For the average woman who needs a practical approach to self-defense, such an expenditure of time and effort is neither productive nor necessary.

In addition, training in a specific Martial Art form for any extended period of time may be very expensive. There are, however, some aspects of the various forms of Martial Arts programs that can be applied to a practical program of self-defense for women. *Self-Defense for Women: The West Point Way* incorporates these aspects into easily understood techniques that can be employed by women of all ages.

The First Step

The initial step in the struggle for survival is to commit yourself to doing everything possible to lead a long and injury-free life. Undeniably, this commitment begins with the learning of techniques for self-defense, so turn now to Chapter 2 and begin the program that may save your life. Don't delay! The urban jungle is becoming more dangerous *everyday!*

2 Basic Principles of Self-Defense

This chapter covers the personal weapons of the body, vulnerable areas of the body and methods of attack, the basic defensive stance, falling techniques, the ground defense position and finally the four basic steps in self-defense for women.

When a woman is attacked, she normally will have to rely on her own body's personal weapons to defend herself. It is to her advantage to know where these weapons are located and to understand how best to use them. If another and better weapon does happen to be available (i.e., a chair, purse, belt, rock, bottle, etc.), the victim should—by all means—use it! However, it is not recommended that the woman carry or attempt to use commercial-type weapons, such as a gun or knife. These could be taken away from the victim and used by the assailant on the victim *herself*.

Every female should remember that in self-defense, there is no such thing as fair play. In a life-and-death situation, any act of defense that might work should be attempted. Know the personal weapons of the body as well as your own potential to use them in self-defense. Among the personal weapons of the body are:

> *Head*: (1) Strike with forehead and (2) base of the skull
> *Mouth*: Talk, shout and bite
> *Hand Strikes*: (3) fist, (4) bottom fist, (5) knife edge, (6) two or more extended knuckles, (7) palm heel, (8) spear hand, and fingers (scratch, jab, gouge, pinch)
> *Foot kicks*: (9) side, (10) ball and (11) heel of the foot. Also toes if shoes are worn.
> *Knee* (12) Knee-up kick
> *Elbow* (13) jab to rear

Vulnerable Areas of the Body and Methods of Attack

There are certain vulnerable or exposed parts of the body that are particularly susceptible to external blows or pressure and that when attacked properly will cause the assailant a great deal of pain. By attacking these areas, a woman can lessen the effectiveness of an opponent's hold or attack. Learning how to attack these areas correctly is one of the *most important* elements of any woman's self-defense training. If she does nothing else, a woman who can quickly react to an attack situation with an immediate and aggressive counterattack to exposed areas will have an excellent chance of never

1. FOREHEAD STRIKE   2. BASE OF SKULL

3. HAND—FIST (PUNCH)

4. HAND—BOTTOM FIST

5. HAND—KNIFE EDGE

6. HAND—EXTENDED KNUCKLES

7. HAND—PALM HEEL

8. HAND—SPEAR HAND

9. FOOT—
SIDE OF FOOT

10. FOOT—
BALL OF FOOT

11. FOOT—
HEEL OF FOOT

12. KNEE—KNEE-UP KICK

13. ELBOW—JAB TO REAR

becoming another statistic—a victim of rape or some other violent crime.

The skills required to attack these areas are neither difficult to learn, nor do they require a great deal of strength to be effective. Speed and accuracy, however, as opposed to brute strength or size, are essential prerequisites.

A few of the self-defense "attack methods" may seem too cruel and vicious to some women. They should remember that, in most instances, rape and sexual assault is in fact a life-or-death confrontation. Once the decision has been made to react with a counterattack, the effort must be 100 percent with full force. The counterattack may be an attack to a vulnerable area, or a series of blows to many areas. The assailant must be sufficiently hurt or startled to allow the victim time to release herself from a hold, if necessary, and escape to safety. A halfhearted, unsuccessful act of self-defense can easily result in further angering the assailant, who will then try harder to subdue his victim.

A quick reaction or distraction is an effort by the victim to divert the assailant from his assault. Although screaming may be one type of reaction, the primary method of distracting is to commit a painful act on the assailant by attacking vulnerable areas of his body. Distractions are intended to either cause the assailant to immediately release his hold on the victim, or momentarily startle the assailant in order to provide the victim with the additional time needed to complete her release.

A retaliation is another response in a victim's arsenal of self-defense actions. *After* a successful release from a hold, and as the victim is escaping, she may wish to further expand her defense by attacking her assailant's vulnerable areas again (a retaliation). A retaliation should be a quick attack and should be used to discourage the assailant from attacking or grabbing the victim again. For example, after a release from a front choke, the victim delivers a side snap kick to the assailant's knee as she is escaping or running away!

Probably the five most vulnerable or exposed areas of the body to attack are the eyes, groin, neck, knee and nose. The main vulnerable areas of the body and the appropriate methods of attack are:

1. Front of Body:
    a. *Eyes*: (14) fingers jab, (15) thumb gouge, scratch
    b. *Hair*: pull or jerk
    c. *Temples* (16) knuckle punch
    d. *Nose*: (17) palm heel underneath, (18) bottom fist, (19) knife edge hand to bridge, (20) forehead and (21) base of skull strike to bridge of nose
    e. *Lips*: (22) finger pinch, twist and rip. Also knuckle punch to upper lip (23)
    f. *Ears* (24) pop with cupped hands, bite
    g. *Chin* (25) palm heel underneath
    h. *Mastoid Process* (26) thumb jab and lift at the mastoid process
    i. *Throat*: Adam's apple, carotid arteries, windpipe: (27) knife edge hand, (28) spear hand, (29) knuckle jab, and (30) gag reflex on front of neck (below Adam's apple)
    j. *Clavicle*: (31) knife edge hand, (32) bottom fist
    k. *Armpit*: pinch and twist
    l. *Solar Plexus* (right below sternum): (33) palm heel, (34) punch, (35) elbow jab
    m. *Floating ribs*: (36) elbow jab, (37) punch

n. *Groin*: (38) kick, (39) knee-up, (40) punch, (41) elbow jab, (42) knife edge hand, and (43) testicle pull and twist
o. *Wrist* (44) counter joint action
p. *Fingers* (45) counter joint action
q. *Inner-thigh*: pinch and twist
r. *Knee*: (46) front kick to patella (kneecap), (47) side kick to front, and (48) side
s. *Shins*: (49) front kick and (50) scrape
t. *Instep* (51) heel stomp

2. Rear of Body:

a. *Base of skull* (52) palm heel
b. *Neck*: (53) knife edge hand, (54) punch
c. *Shoulder* (55) counter joint action
d. *Elbow* (56) counter joint action
e. *Back of hand* (57) knuckle punch
f. *Kidneys*: (58) punch, (59) kick
g. *Tailbone* (60) kick
h. *Achilles Tendon* (61) kick
i. *Back of knee* (62) kick

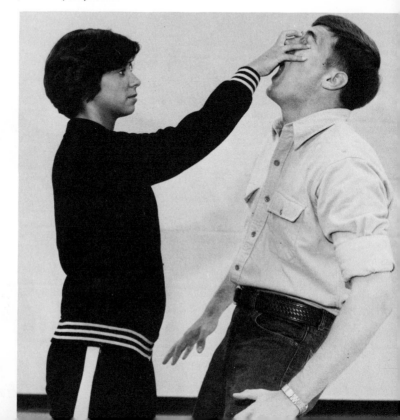

14. EYES—
FINGER JAB

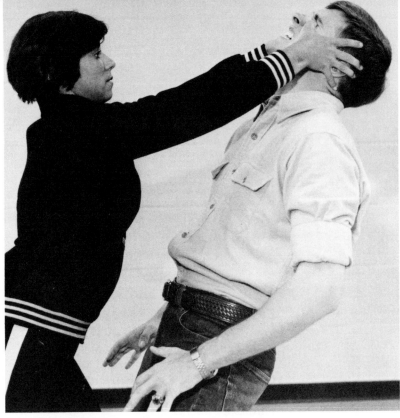

15. EYES—THUMB GOUGE

16. TEMPLE—KNUCKLE PUNCH

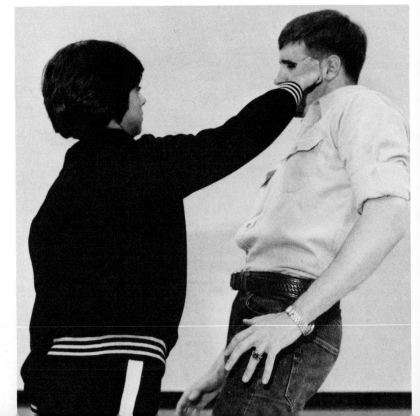

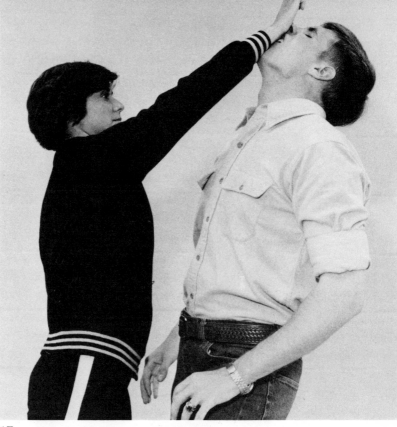

17. NOSE—PALM HEEL UNDERNEATH

18. NOSE—BOTTOM FIST ON BRIDGE

19. NOSE—KNIFE EDGE ON BRIDGE

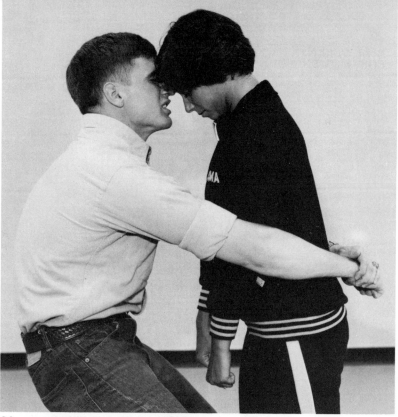

20. NOSE—FOREHEAD ON BRIDGE

21. NOSE—BASE OF SKULL ON BRIDGE

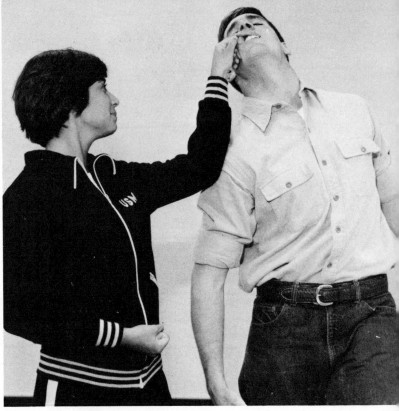

22. LIPS—FINGER PINCH AND TWIST

23. UPPER LIP—KNUCKLE PUNCH

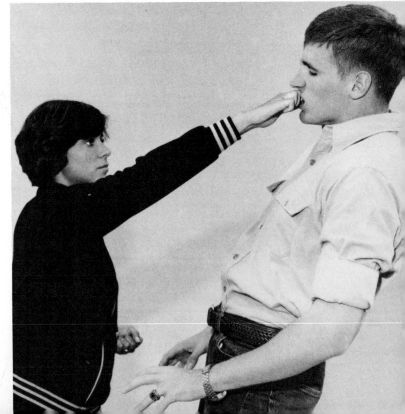

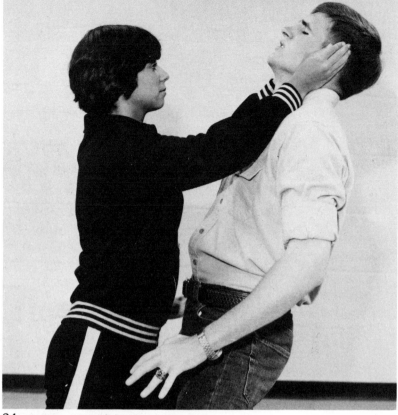

24. EARS—CUPPED HANDS OVER EARS

25. CHIN—PALM HEEL UNDERNEATH

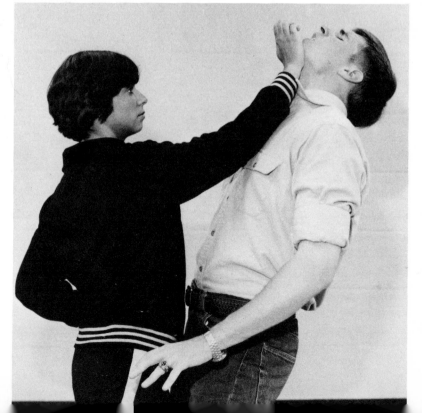

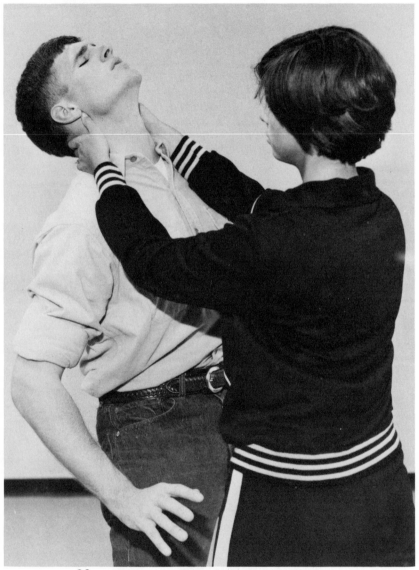

26. MASTOID PROCESS—LIFT UP

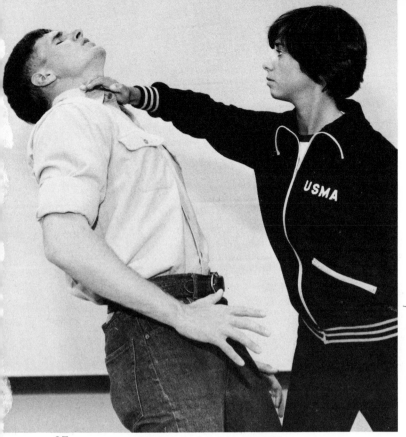

27. **THROAT—KNIFE EDGE HAND STRIKE**

28. **THROAT—SPEAR HAND STRIKE**

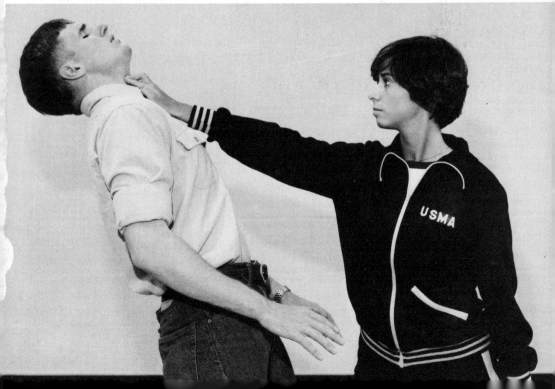

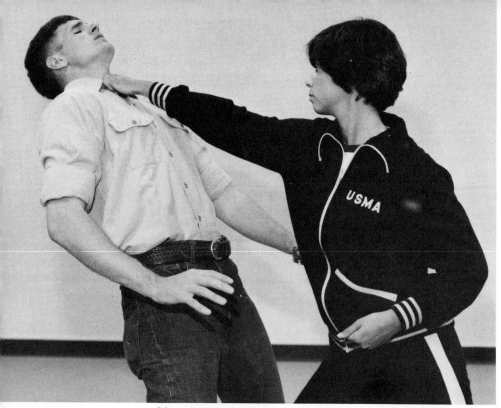

29. **THROAT—KNUCKLE PUNCH**

30. **THROAT—GAG REFLEX ATTACK**

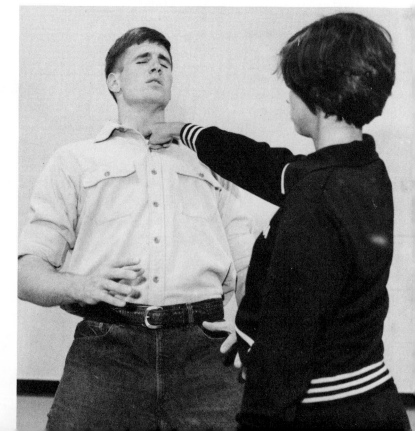

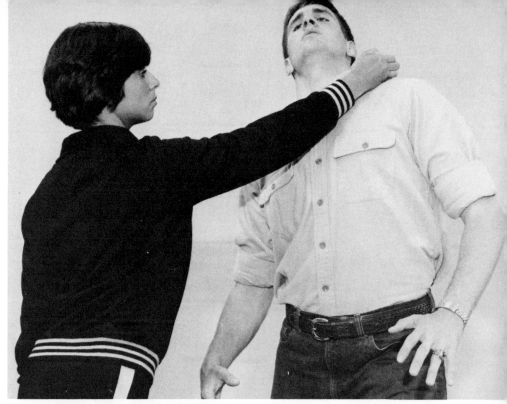

31. **CLAVICLE—KNIFE EDGE STRIKE**

32. **CLAVICLE—BOTTOM FIST STRIKE**

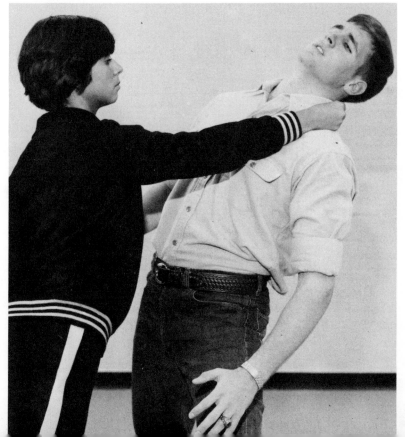

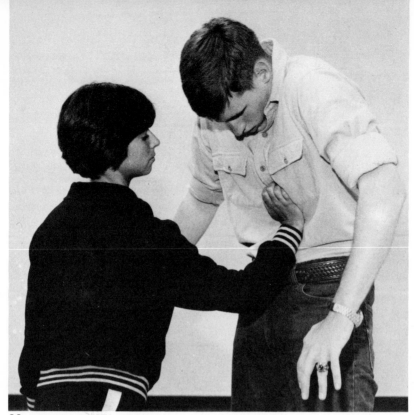

33. **SOLAR PLEXUS—PALM HEEL STRIKE**

34. **SOLAR PLEXUS—FIST PUNCH**

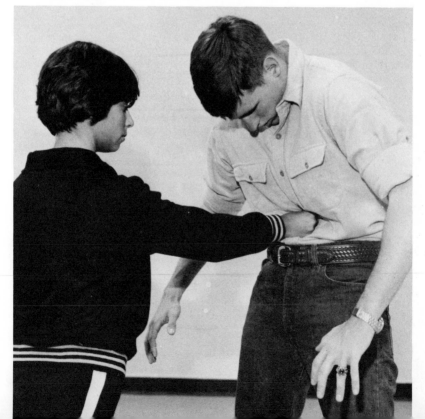

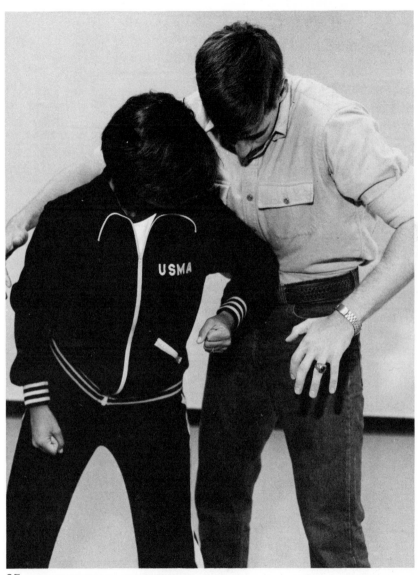

35. SOLAR PLEXUS—ELBOW JAB

36. FLOATING RIBS—ELBOW JAB

37. FLOATING RIBS—FIST PUNCH

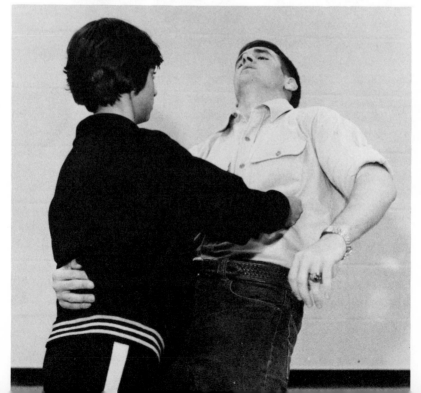

38. GROIN—FRONT KICK

39. GROIN—KNEE-UP KICK

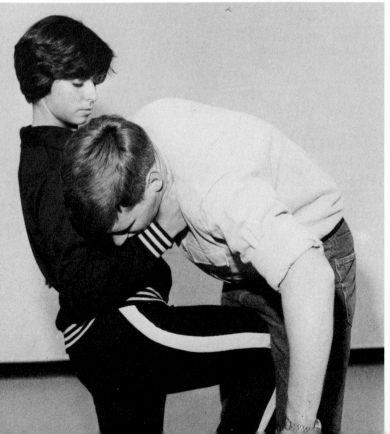

40. **GROIN—FIST PUNCH**

41. **GROIN—ELBOW JAB**

42. GROIN—KNIFE EDGE STRIKE

43. GROIN—TESTICLE PULL

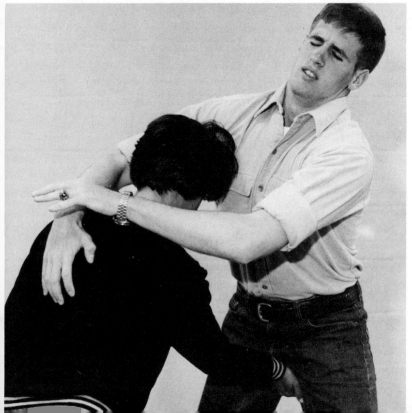

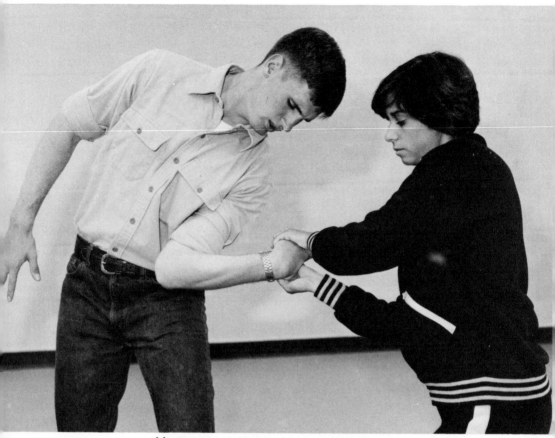

44. WRIST—COUNTER JOINT ACTION

45. FINGER—COUNTER JOINT ACTION

46. FRONT KNEE—FRONT KICK

47. FRONT KNEE—SIDE KICK

48. SIDE KNEE—SIDE KICK

49. SHINS—FRONT KICK

50. SHINS—SCRAPE

51. INSTEP—FOOT STOMP

52. BASE OF SKULL—PALM HEEL STRIKE

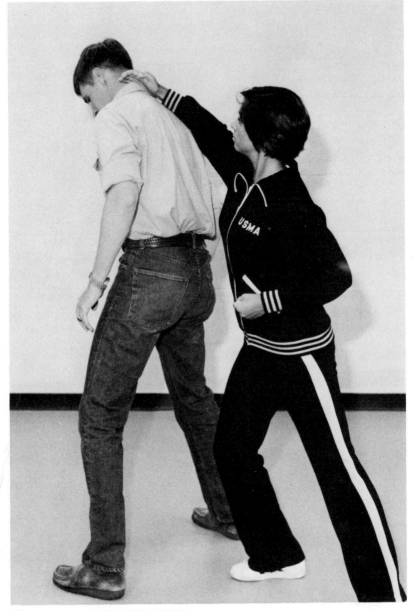

53. NECK—KNIFE EDGE STRIKE

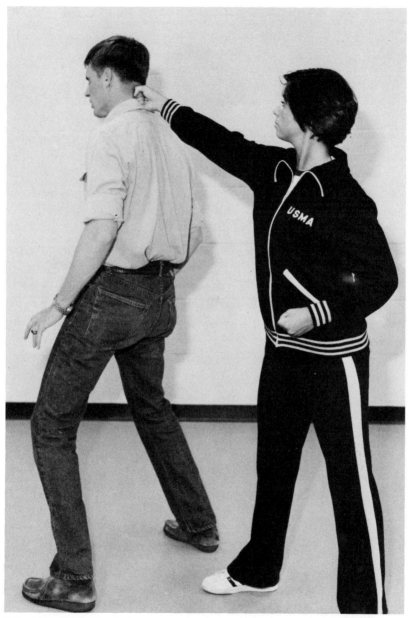

54. NECK—FIST PUNCH

55. SHOULDER—COUNTER JOINT ACTION

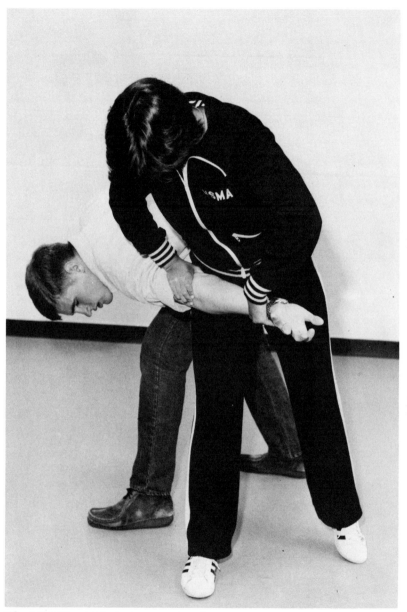

56. ELBOW—COUNTER JOINT ACTION

57. BACK OF HAND—KNUCKLE PUNCH

58. **KIDNEYS—FIST PUNCH**

59. KIDNEYS—KICK

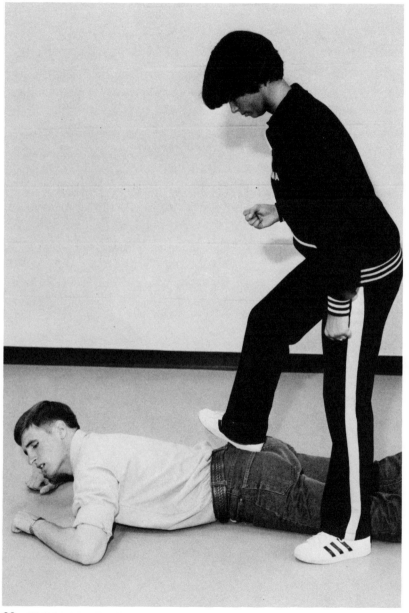

60. TAILBONE—KICK OR FOOT STOMP

61. ACHILLES TENDON—KICK

62. BACK OF KNEE—KICK

Basic Defensive Stance

For a potential victim, the best position for self-defense is a standing position with the assailant to the front. Once the victim is either on the ground or the attack is from a rearward direction, defending herself becomes a much more difficult task. As well as providing the best position for self-protection, assuming a good basic defensive stance will demonstrate self-confidence. The defensive stance should protect the

63. DEFENSIVE STANCE—RIGHT

most vital parts of the body from attack and enable one to move quickly in any direction—either to escape or counterattack. But do not assume a full defensive stance until you know what you need to defend yourself. Do not appear to be threatening unless you have already been threatened! (See pictures 63 and 64.)

BODY POSITION: The body is turned so either side faces the opponent. This position protects the vital organs that are located principally in the front of the

64. DEFENSIVE STANCE—LEFT

body, and also provides a smaller target area to the assailant.

FOOT POSITION: The feet are approximately shoulder width apart with one slightly behind the other (45-degree angle to the other). The knees are slightly bent (Do not lock the knees—this inhibits movement). Body weight is evenly distributed on both feet so quick movement can be made in any direction.

ARM AND HAND POSITION: The hands are held in a closed or slightly open fist. One arm is held high, away from the body, nearest the opponent, primarily to protect the face. The elbow is bent and pointing downward, and held in close to the body to protect the ribs. The other arm is farthest from the opponent and with the elbow bent is held lower than the other arm. The hand is in a central position over the solar plexus and moves quickly up or down to protect the face, heart, and groin.

Falling

Knowing how to fall correctly is very important if the victim trips during a struggle, or is pushed or thrown to the ground by the assailant. The almost instinctive, protective tendency to tense up, and put out a hand or foot to break the fall, should be avoided. Many unnecessary injuries happen to people who fall in this manner. You have to land safely and be able to recover to a standing position as soon as possible.

Once the victim starts falling, she should try to relax and let more than one part of her body absorb the impact of the fall. The best way to do this is to try to roll out of the fall, protecting one's head by holding it

65. SQUAT FALL—STARTING POSITION

66. SQUAT FALL—LANDING POSITION

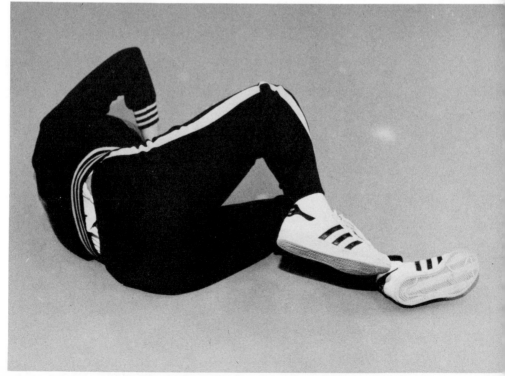

to one side with the chin tucked to the chest. The roll is generally diagonally across the shoulder and back and should enable a person to return to an upright position.

Learning to fall correctly may be very difficult for some women. It is important to keep the technique simple—like this basic somersault or shoulder roll. Initial practice should be on a mat or other padded surface. It should progress from a stationary squat position to a moving upright position with 2 or 3 steps taken before the fall. (See pictures 65 and 66, squat start and finish.)

Side and rear Judo falls are also effective but require more skill and practice time to perform properly. (See pictures 67 and 68.)

67. SIDE FALL

while the free hand is held up by the face. This position will keep the vital areas away from the attacker, and protect the face and front parts of the body. If the attacker moves toward the front vital areas, quickly flip over onto the other side, so the buttocks are always toward the attacker. (See picture 69 with assailant.)

• *Legs*: Use kicks at all times to attack and ward off the assailant. Use quick, front and side snap kicks so your foot cannot be grabbed. As soon as possible, slide or scoot back away from the assailant and get up to a standing position. (See picture 70.) Keep the assailant to your front at all times.

• *Practice*:

    a. Alone: Step back and fall down to the floor, assume a ground defensive position; kick out and recover to the basic defensive stance as quickly as possible. Initially, practice on a rug or padded surface.

    b. With a partner: Partner pushes you down and tries to grab a foot or leg; perform as instructed.

Four Basic Steps in Self-Defense

STEP ONE: Avoid a potentially dangerous situation if at all possible;

STEP TWO: Attempt to *Run* to safety if cover or assistance appears to be near. Do not run just to be chased and then caught while out of breath;

STEP THREE: Attract attention by *Shouting* for help if potential assistance might be near. (i.e., Cry "FIRE!"); and

STEP FOUR: Develop and employ, when necessary, appropriate *Self-Defense* techniques.

68. REAR FALL

Ground Defense

If pushed or pulled to the ground and unable to recover immediately to a standing position, the victim should assume a ground defense. This is only held until recovery to the basic (standing) defensive stance can be accomplished.

Sit with your weight over one side of the body, with the bottom leg slightly bent and the top leg bent and ready to kick. The torso is supported up on one hand,

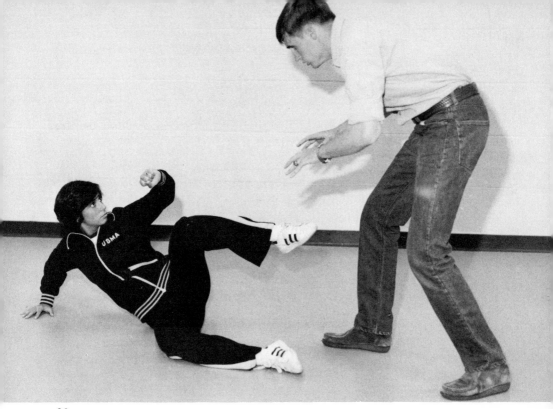

69. GROUND DEFENSE WITH ATTACKER

70. GROUND DEFENSE—GETTING UP TO FEET

A basic self-defense program includes working on the following 4 "R's":

React: Prior to attempting release, quickly distract by attacking vulnerable areas of the body.

Release: The method or technique used to escape the hold.

Retaliate: As you escape, be ready to attack vulnerable areas again.

Run: Immediately run from the opponent to safety. *Do Not* give the assailant a chance to attack or grab you again. The second attempt may be more dangerous!

3 Fitness and Self-Defense

A self-defense program for women is not realistic unless physical fitness is a part of it. A woman who hopes to learn, practice and successfully use (when necessary) the self-defense skills found in this book should be physically fit. Although numerous definitions of fitness exist, in the case of self-defense, physical fitness is the capacity of an individual to successfully meet a *physical* challenge.* At the minimum, a physically fit woman should possess a reasonably high level of each of the basic components of fitness: cardiovascular fitness, flexibility and muscular fitness. Cardiovascular fitness is the ability of the body to continue prolonged activity while resisting fatigue. Flexibility refers to an increased range of motion of the skeletal

* For a more extensive discussion of physical fitness and personal conditioning programs, refer to *Conditioning for a Purpose*, James A. Peterson, Ph.D., editor (Leisure Press, West Point, New York 10996), 1977.

joints of the body, which allows improved movement. Muscular fitness is the capacity of the body to exert force against resistance. Without these basic components of physical fitness, a victim has considerably less of a chance of successfully warding off the average male attacker.

The following exercises are designed to improve and contribute to the basic components of personal fitness. Physical exercise and activity should be an integral part of *every* woman's daily life. It may take many forms: individual lifetime sports, such as tennis, golf and racquetball; recreation exercising, such as jogging, swimming, and bicycling; or, finally, specific developmental exercising, such as calisthenics.

A developmental exercise program should be performed at least three to four times a week, and more frequently if possible. A workout should last at least fifteen to twenty minutes. Prior to beginning any type of exercise program, a *physician* should be consulted regarding the ability of the individual to engage in the proposed exercise program.

In some instances, an extensive physical examination may be necessary before the exercise program commences. A developmental workout should give attention to all three major components of physical fitness. In order to ensure that the individual has a proper foundation of fitness, the workouts and conditioning efforts can be segmented into three levels of performance: beginner; intermediate; and advanced. The beginner's level of exercise is for the individual who is just starting an exercise program; the intermediate level is for someone who has been doing some form of regular exercise or physical activity; and the advanced exercises are for the individual who exercises vigorously almost daily.

Cardiovascular Fitness

This type of exercise must be vigorous enough to require both the heart and the lungs to work at a greater-than-resting level of efficiency. Physical activities, such as running, jogging, swimming, jumping, skipping rope and/or bicycling, are large-muscle activities that will help the individual develop her level of cardiovascular fitness. The following specific exercises will also contribute to muscular endurance and should be performed as warm-ups prior to doing strength and flexibility type exercises:

BEGINNER

1. Run in place 50 counts (25 counts on each foot) with hands on hips or arms bent loosely at elbows, raising knees up waist high (71). Continue with 10 jumping jacks: from a standing position, with legs together, jump with legs apart and hands clapping overhead (72), and return to start by bringing legs together again as hands slap thighs (73). Relax and repeat the 50 count running in place and ten jumping jacks.

OR

2. Jump in place with hands on hips and feet together first forward, then backward, then right and left. Repeat series in that order fifteen to twenty times. Relax and repeat sequence once again.

71. RUNNING IN PLACE

72. JUMPING JACKS—
CLAPPING HANDS POSITION

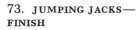

73. JUMPING JACKS—
FINISH

INTERMEDIATE

1. Run in place 100 counts; continue with 15 jumping jacks. Relax and repeat sequence once again.

OR

2. Jump in place forward, backward, right and left 50 counts. Relax and repeat once again.

OR

3. Jump rope in place with feet together 100 counts. Relax and repeat once again. (74)

ADVANCED

1. Run in place 2 to 3 minutes. Relax, repeat once again.

OR

2. Jump rope 2 to 3 minutes. Relax, repeat once again.

OR

3. Do combination jumping jacks: do a jumping jack, then quickly kick the right leg up high to the left while clapping hands together under leg, quickly repeat kick with left leg to right and clap hands. (75) Do this combination 20 times. Relax, repeat sequence once again.

74. ROPE JUMPING

75. COMBINATION
JUMPING JACK

Flexibility

The following flexibility exercises concentrate on stretching the back, trunk, legs, arms and shoulders. The exercises are performed *slowly* and *smoothly*. Each static stretch is held 2 to 3 seconds—do not bounce while doing these exercises. Stretching exercises should be done prior to strengthening-type exercises.

BEGINNER (Perform each of the following exercises 6 to 8 times.)

1. Leg flexibility series—Sitting position: Sit with extended legs together—slowly bend forward and try to touch chest to thighs with hands reaching to ankles. If you can't make it, go as far as you can (76). Each day you'll improve. That is invariably true of progress on flexibility exercises, and is applicable to all that follows in this section. Hold 2 to 3 seconds. Relax, repeat.

76. SEATED LEG FLEXIBILITY—LEGS TOGETHER

- Sit with legs apart; turn to left and try to touch chest to thighs, hands reaching to ankle. (77) Reach center with both hands (78), and then turn right and touch. Return center, relax and repeat left, center, right.

77. **SEATED LEG FLEXIBILITY—LEGS APART WITH SIDE TOUCH**

78. **SEATED LEG FLEXIBILITY—LEGS APART WITH CENTER TOUCH**

79. SEATED LEG FLEXIBILITY—FROG SIT TOUCH

80. SEATED LEG FLEXIBILITY—HURDLE POSITION

- Sit with legs bent and soles of feet together. Hands grasp ankles. Bend at waist moving chest forward and downward pushing head toward ankles. (79) Hold, 2 to 3 seconds, return up and repeat.
- Hurdle sit: Left leg extended forward and right leg bent backward. Turn left and try to touch chest to thigh—with hands reaching to ankle, hold (80); return up, change hurdle position and repeat to right. Continue left and right, etc.
2. Arm flings: Sit with legs crossed and back straight. Bend the arms and hold up at shoulder level, with fingertips just about touching (81).

81. ARM FLING—STARTING POSITION

82. ARM FLING—FINISH

Pull bent arms backward 3 counts (1001, 1002, 1003) and on 4th count fling the arms, elbows extended fully, backward (82). Repeat sequence. Keep arms up at shoulder level throughout exercises.

INTERMEDIATE AND ADVANCED (Perform each of the following exercises 8 to 10 times unless otherwise instructed.)

    1. Leg flexibility series:
- *Standing position*:
        1. Legs extended with knees straight and to-gether, bend at waist and touch toes with both hands (83). Hold 2 to 3 seconds, relax, repeat.

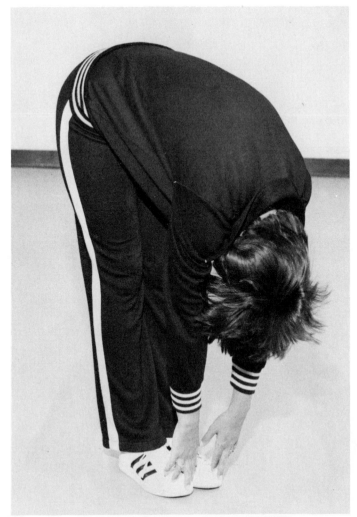

83. **STANDING LEG FLEXIBILITY—LEGS TOGETHER**

84. STANDING LEG FLEXIBILITY—LEGS APART, SIDE TOUCH

85. STANDING LEG FLEXIBILITY—LEGS APART, CENTER TOUCH

2. Legs extended and apart, turn to left and touch both hands to left anklebone and hold (84); move to center and touch both hands to floor and hold (85); move to right and touch both hands to right anklebone, hold 2 to 3 seconds. Return upright and repeat, left, center, right, etc.

• *Sitting position*: See Beginner's exercises

2. Arm Circles: From a standing position, arms at sides, full circle the left arm 10 counts forward (86), 10 backward; then right arm 10

86. STANDING SINGLE ARM CIRCLES—FIST

forward and 10 backward; and both arms together 10 forward and 10 backward. Relax and
repeat sequence once again.

- *Variation*: Arms held out at shoulder level with
hands in a fist, quickly describe large circle with
both arms. 10 counts forward and 10 backward
(87). Relax, repeat once again.

87. **STANDING DOUBLE ARM CIRCLES—FISTS**

Muscular Fitness

The following muscular fitness exercises concentrate on the abdominal, leg/hips, and arm/shoulder girdle areas. These body areas generally lack firmness and muscle tonus. The exercises are performed slowly and smoothly. For this exercise usually the count will be 2 (1001, 1002) for upward movement; 4 counts (1001, 1002, 1003, 1004) for a downward movement. A held position is usually for 2 to 3 seconds. These exercises should be performed after warm-up and flexibility exercises.

BEGINNER (Perform each of the following exercises 6 to 8 times):

1. Abdominal:
    a. Curl-ups: Lie on back, with knees slightly bent, fingers interlaced behind neck. Slowly curl head (tucking chin to chest) forward and continue curling upward until head and shoulders are off floor (88); hold and slowly uncurl downward. Relax, and repeat.
    b. Hip roll (Abdominal and trunk strength): Lie on back with arms held out at sides.

88. CURL-UP

89. HIP ROLL TO SIDE

Slowly bring both knees up to chest, roll right with knees pointed toward elbow and lower knees until 1 to 2 inches from floor (89); hold. Return center, roll left and hold; return center and extend legs to starting position. Relax, repeat. Keep head, shoulders and upper back on floor as much as possible.

2. Legs and hips:
   a. Hand-knee leg lift: Kneeling on hands and knees, extend right leg backward along floor and slowly lift 10 to 12 inches. Hold and slowly lower but do not touch floor (90). Repeat in succession. Repeat with left leg. Do not lift leg higher than hips.
   b. Side leg lift: Lie on side with one leg on top of the other. Slowly lift one leg 8 to 10 inches only (91) and hold, and slowly lower but do not touch lower leg. Repeat in suc-

90. **HAND KNEE LEG LIFT**

91. **SINGLE SIDE LYING LEG LIFT**

cession. Roll onto other side and repeat with other leg. Keep body in a straight line.

c. Wall sit: Sit against a wall with feet flat on the floor, back and shoulders pressed tight against wall with hands resting on thighs (92). Hold sitting position 15 to 30 seconds and increase to one minute.

3. Arms and shoulders:

a. This is an isometric pull and push exercise. Sitting comfortably, arms held out and elbows bent, grasp fingertips together and pull one against the other as hard as possible for

92. WALL SIT

93. **ISOMETRIC HAND PULL**

94. **ISOMETRIC HAND PUSH**

95. WALL PUSH—2 HANDS

96. WALL PUSH—1 HAND

4 to 6 seconds (93). Relax, and shake loose. Then place heels of hands together with fingers extended in opposite directions (94) and push hard together for 4 to 6 seconds. Shake hands loose for relaxation and repeat.

b. Wall push: Stand approximately arm's distance from a wall with hands placed on wall at or just above eye level, fingertips touching. Keep heels on floor and body straight. Move body toward wall with arms bending until forehead touches hands (95). Push against wall and extend arms, moving body slowly backwards to starting position. Repeat.

Variation: Do first with right arm only, and then with left arm only (96).

INTERMEDIATE (Perform each of the following exercises 8 to 12 times unless otherwise instructed):

1. Abdominals:
   a. Sit-ups: Lie on back with knees bent and hands clasped behind head. Slowly curl forward and upward until chest touches knees,

97. SIT-UP

98. HIP ROLL EXTENSION TO SIDE

and then uncurl slowly backward to start. Repeat (97).

b. Hip Roll variation (abdominal and trunk): Lie on back with arms held out at sides. Bend knees to chest, roll right with knees pointed toward elbow, and lower knees 1 to 2 inches from floor. Quickly extend legs diagonally to right and hold 2 to 3 counts (98). Bend knees and return center, roll left, extend legs and hold 2 to 3 counts, return center. Relax and repeat.

2. Legs and hips:

a. Lateral leg lift: Kneeling on hands and knees, lift right bent knee up to side (99), extend right leg out laterally (100), quickly

99. **LATERAL LEG LIFT—BENT LEG POSITION**

100. **LATERAL LEG LIFT—EXTENDED LEG POSITION**

return to bent knee position and back to
start. Now do the same with left leg. Repeat.
   b. Hand-knee leg lift variation: On hands and
knees with toes pointed, extend right leg
backward along floor, slowly lift leg 10 to 12
inches, hold and describe 6 small circles
with that leg. Slowly lower but do not touch
floor; lift and repeat. Do the same with left
leg, and repeat.
3. Arms and shoulders:
   a. Push-ups: With body supported up on fully
extended arms and toes (101), slowly lower

101. PUSH UP—STARTING POSITION

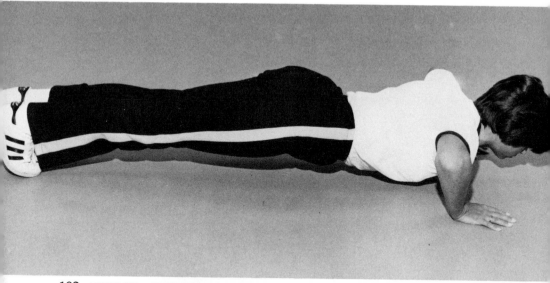

102. PUSH UP—LOWERED POSITION

chest almost to floor by bending elbows
(102), return to start by straightening elbows. Keep back straight and head up. Do
not let hips or thighs touch floor. If none
or only a few of these push-ups can be
done properly, try to do *negative* push-ups:
lower chest to floor very slowly (6 counts)
and then rest momentarily, letting body
touch down to floor. As quickly as possible,
recover to start position *not* relying on push-
up with the arms, but making it easier by
transferring weight momentarily to thighs
and knees. Now, back in the start position,
repeat exercise.

103. SEATED DOUBLE ARM CIRCLES—PALMS UP

b. Arms circles: Sitting comfortably with arms
extended out to sides. Turn palms upward
and slowly describe large circles with arms
(103), 10 forward and 10 backward. Relax,
repeat.
Variation: Circle rapidly—10 forward and
10 backward describing very small circles.

ADVANCED (Perform each of the following exercises 12 to 15 times):

1. Abdominals:
   a. Double leg lift: Lie on back with shoulders raised and upper body supported on forearms. Keeping lower back in contact with floor, raise both extended legs only about 10 to 12 inches off floor. Slowly lower to floor but do not touch down (104). Repeat slowly in succession. Be sure to breathe throughout exercise and do not arch lower back!
   b. Trunk-rotating sit-ups (abdominal and trunk): Sitting with knees bent and hands clasped behind neck, rotate right (105) as

104. DOUBLE LEG LIFT

far as possible and slowly uncurl backwards but do not touch floor. Keep rotating and slowly curl upward to start. Now rotate left, and repeat exercise, then repeat alternately, right and left.

2. Legs and hips:

a. Combination side leg lift: Lying on left side (108), slowly raise right leg 8 to 10 inches and hold. Then raise left leg to meet right leg and hold. Don't bend knees. Slowly lower both legs to starting position and repeat. Roll over to right side and do exercise in reverse.

b. Flutter kick: Lie on your front with head resting on crossed arms. Lift both legs together off floor, knees straight, and flutter kick (107), 6 counts. Lower to start, relax and repeat. (Keep head down.) Do not arch back.

105. TRUNK ROTATING SIT-UP

106. **COMBINATION SIDE LYING LEG LIFT**

107. **FLUTTER KICK**

    c. Wall Sit variation: While holding the sitting position against the wall, extend left leg out in front and slowly lift and lower (108). Return to start and repeat with right leg, left, right, left, right, etc.

3. Arms: Repeat Intermediate exercises for arms.

108. WALL SIT WITH EXTENDED LEG

4 Prevention

Hundreds of women are robbed, mugged, sexually assaulted and even raped everyday in the United States. Every woman is a potential victim. Many of these crimes could be prevented if women used some common sense measures and simple safeguards. This chapter discusses safety for the individual in her home, in her car, and on the street.

Personal Safety

An attacker will most often select a victim who is highly vulnerable. On the contrary, a woman, regardless of age, who is alert, confident and in good physical condition is less likely to be a victim. At all times be conscious of how you look and act. Dress appropriately. When alone, wear comfortable clothing and if possible, shoes appropriate for running or quick movement. Have confidence in your physical, as well as mental, capabilities and stamina. Always be alert to your surroundings and be aware of the people who are around you at all times. Do not fall asleep or daydream. Remain calm if confronted with a dangerous situation. Don't panic! Whenever there is a possibility of attack, be prepared mentally, as well as physically. Know ahead of time exactly what you would do in a specific hazardous situation.

Be prepared to employ either your purse itself or items in it to ward off an attacker. If an attack is feared, have a purse weapon in your hand and be ready to use it. Several items typically contained in a purse make good weapons for jabbing, stabbing or slashing at vulnerable parts of the attacker's body.
A few examples are:

> comb: stab eyes or throat; scrape face;
> brush: jab pointed end to throat, hit groin;
> keys: stab eyes, throat;
> pen or pencil (or metal nail file): jab or stab, at face or back of hand;
> hairspray (or breath spray): spray it into eyes; whistle: blow in ear or to call for help; or sling or throw entire purse or individual items within it at assailant.

Safety at Home

Many crimes occur in the victim's home. The following precautions should be taken for safety there:

1. Keep the doors locked at all times—whether home or not.
2. Use good locks—i.e., dead bolt. Use a chain lock and if possible a peephole in the door. Be sure to check to see who is at the door *before* opening it.
3. Lock and secure screen and windows if accessible (even in summer).

4. Keep shades, curtains, and drapes closed—especially when dressing.

5. Never admit a stranger. Ask to see appropriate identification for a salesman, repairman, and/or delivery man. If necessary, make a phone call to check if that person was actually sent to your home.

6. If a stranger asks to use the phone, ask for the number and you call while he waits outside.

7. Make sure all entrances to your residence are well lighted. When returning home after dark, be sure a light is on at that entrance.

8. Install an automatic timer to turn lights on at dusk when you are away. Lights tend to discourage intruders.

9. Do not make it known to strangers that you will be home alone on a particular night. If a stranger does knock at the door, make him think you are *not* alone. Yell, "John, get the door, I'm busy." or, "My brother will be with you in a minute," etc.

10. Be careful in choosing where to hide an extra key. Robbers know to look under the doormat or on the ledge above the door.

11. If you live in a high crime rate area, install warning devices or have a dog who will bark at strangers. This does not need to be a trained "killer" dog.

12. Keep a phone beside the bed (or easily within reach).

13. When returning home at night, have your keys unobtrusively out in your hand before reaching the door. Do not call attention that you're returning to an empty home.

14. If upon returning home you suspect a prowler

is inside, leave and obtain help. Do not enter alone!

15. If you are inside your home and you hear someone else in the house, remain calm, and call the police or fire department. Do not try to confront him . . . he may have a weapon.

16. If on vacation or away for a couple of days, secure the home and stop regular deliveries such as the newspaper or milk. Ask a friend to pick up mail and to watch your home while you are gone. You may also wish to leave on (or use an automatic timer) a light or a radio so it appears someone is home.

17. If you receive an obscene phone call:
hang up immediately;
if calls continue, notify police and phone company.
There is some point in blowing a whistle into the phone.
Do not try to counsel the caller.
Do not give your number to a person who says he has the wrong number. Ask what number he wants and say, no—this is not your number.
Do not let the caller know you are alone.

Safety in a Car

The following precautions should be taken:

1. Keep all doors and windows closed and locked. If a window must be opened, open it on the driver's side only, just enough for air.

2. Use well-lighted streets and thoroughfares. Do not take shortcuts on unknown roads, or lonely roads without traveler's services.

3. Always keep your car locked. Park in areas that will be well lighted when you return to your car. Have your key ready in your hand and check the front and rear to be sure no one is hiding inside before you enter the car.
4. Do not pick up hitchhikers!
5. Before departing on a trip, be sure everything is in working order—i.e., that you have plenty of gas, water, a spare tire and flares.
6. If the car breaks down, put on your flashers, raise the hood, and remain in the locked car. If a motorist stops to help, ask him to call the police or a tow truck. Do not get out of the car (day or night).
7. Do not leave your keys with a parking attendant (your car key as well as any other key on the ring may be duplicated in a very short time). If you must leave the car keys, leave *only* the ignition key. Do not mark your key ring with your name, address or phone number.
8. If you believe you are being followed, drive to a police station or to a gas station. Do not drive home.
9. If you get home and discover you have been followed, stay in the locked car. Blow the horn to attract attention or drive to safety if possible. Do not leave the car.
10. Always carry change in the car for a phone call.

Safety on the Street

If walking day or night, the following precautions should be taken:

1. If at all possible, avoid walking alone (especially after dark). There is safety in numbers.
2. If alone, walk briskly and confidently. Be alert and aware of your surroundings.
3. Walk through familiar neighborhoods and on familiar streets. Go where there are streetlights, businesses and people.
4. Avoid taking shortcuts and dark alleys, steer clear of doorways or isolated areas.
5. Walk in the middle of the sidewalk or near the curb if parked cars are not present. Do not walk close to buildings.
6. *Never* hitchhike or accept a ride from strangers (male or female).
7. Avoid talking to strangers. Ignore catcalls, whistles or remarks. If someone in a vehicle asks for directions, keep a safe distance from the person in the car. Do not walk over to the car and possibly get grabbed or pulled inside.
8. Carry change for a phone call, and do notice the location of the police call boxes on the street.
9. If you think you are being followed, make sure. Cross the street, change directions, or enter a business or gas station.
10. If you find you are being followed, stay where you are if you have entered a shop or gas station. Otherwise, blow a whistle or yell for assistance if assistance is near. Since most women would not be able to outrun their assailant, only run from the assailant if help is near or you have someplace to run to.
11. If you are being followed and assistance is not near, stop and face the assailant in a good defensive stance with a purse weapon in hand.

Be confident in your determination to defend yourself.

12. If you are being followed by a car, turn around to walk quickly in the opposite direction. Enter a store, café or gas station and tell someone you are being followed.

13. Keep your hands free. Never overload yourself with packages. If you must defend yourself, either drop all packages or throw them at the assailant.

14. To avoid muggers and purse snatchers:
    Carry your purse close to your body or under your arm—not hanging loosely from the shoulder;
    Do not carry all your money in your purse—distribute it around your person. Do not carry more money than you need.
    Do not leave your purse unattended, i.e., sitting on a counter, or in a shopping basket, or hanging on the back of a door of a public rest room.
    Do not publicly display money or a check, i.e., count your change in the bank or store, not out on the street.
    Do not walk with arms loaded with packages, purse hanging from your arm and keys dangling from your fingers or even teeth toward your home!

15. If someone attempts to rob you, don't be a heroine. If he asks for your valuables give him what he wants. Get a good description of the thief and report the crime to the police immediately—no matter how large or small the value of the items taken.

5 Kicks and Kick Defenses

Basic Kicks: Front, Side and Back

The legs contain some of the most powerful muscles in the body. As a result, leg kicks are one of a woman's best defensive weapons against a variety of frontal or rear attacks. Leg kicks may be used by women of all ages. Since a woman's legs are longer than her arms, the use of her legs enables her to put a greater distance between herself and her opponent than do her hands and arms. Consequently, in most instances, kicking as compared to striking is a much more effective method of self-defense for a woman. Of course, in addition, a woman's shoes usually give added protection. The basic kicks described in this chapter are relatively simple techniques that do not require an extraordinary amount of skill or strength to perform.

GUIDELINES: Generally, kicks should be aimed low. Kicks should rarely be aimed above waist level. Kicks to the head may be effective if done properly, but frequently require too much time to learn and perfect. High-flying karate kicks may look good but are not practical for the average woman to use. Also, it is not very easy for an attacker to grab onto a low kicking leg.

The kicks described in this chapter are always best aimed at vulnerable areas of the body—the shin, knee, or at the highest level, the groin. Kicks are excellent to use as distractions and retaliations because they are performed quickly. If accurate, they can be painful enough to momentarily stun or startle the opponent. In many instances, a kick, skillfully delivered, can catch an attacker by surprise and enable the victim to escape. Be sure to maintain eye contact with the opponent—do not look down at the area to be kicked (this will telegraph the kick). Look the assaulter in the eye and kick him in the knee! In most situations, following the kick, the victim should be prepared to move away quickly and run from the assailant (unless the initial kick fails, in which case it should be followed by another, better, kick!).

FRONT KICK

The front kick is a fast, short kick used for surprise. The kick is aimed primarily at the shin or knee but may also be directed at the groin. The kick starts from the basic defensive stance off of the front foot (either the right or left foot may be the front foot).

• *Starting Position* (109): The body weight is slowly shifted to the rear leg—without making too much movement so that the opponent will not anticipate the kick; then quickly lift the front leg up at the knee (pointing the bent knee at the target).

• *Action* (110): Snap out the leg, kicking with

109. FRONT KICK—
STARTING POSITION

110. FRONT KICK—FINISH

111. FRONT KICK—WITH REAR LEG

the toe of the shoe, the ball of the foot, or the instep if attacking the groin; quickly return to the starting position. Be ready to kick again if necessary. Note: Do not kick with the toes unless shoes are worn which will protect the kicking foot.

• *Variation* (111): The front kick may also be done with the rear leg, which is slower but more powerful. The weight is shifted to the front foot as the rear leg is lifted at the knee and snapped out vigorously.

112. FRONT KICK—PRACTICE WITH PILLOW

• *Practice*: The front kick as well as the other kicks may easily be practiced at home. Place a firm chair cushion or sofa cushion, or a large, firm pillow up against a wall and kick with full force. The cushion or pillow should be large enough so the area kicked is the approximate height of the shin, knee or groin. If a friend or partner is available to help, the cushion or pillow should be held securely in place. Your partner should be careful to stand to the side, out of the way of the kick (112).

Practice single kicks as well as multiple kicks in rapid succession. Practice kicking with both the right and the left leg.

SIDE KICKS

The side snap kick is a very powerful kick aimed at the shin or knee. Since the side of the body is to the opponent throughout the kick, it is often used as the kicker escapes (such as with a retaliation kick).

• *Starting Position*: The kick is from a basic defensive stance—off the front foot. Shift the weight to the rear foot and then lift the knee of the front leg up high so the thigh is parallel to the ground. (113). Shifting the weight backwards is essential in order to get the front leg lifted up high enough and for balance.

• *Action*: Quickly kick out sideways with the leg, driving the heel or side of the foot (not ball of the foot) into attacker's shin or knee (114). Return to starting position and be prepared to escape or kick again if necessary.

113. SIDE KICK—
STARTING POSITION

114. SIDE KICK—FINISH

BACK KICK

Ideally, the victim does not want her back to the opponent. However, if an attack is made from the rear and there is not time to turn and face the opponent, the back kick may be used. A back kick is very powerful, it must be executed quickly and almost instinctively, since the attacker is momentarily out of the line-of-sight of the victim.

• *Starting Position*: The back kick starts from the basic defensive stance using the rear leg. Look back over the same shoulder as the kicking leg— looking over the opposite shoulder will twist the body and cause a weak kick. Looking back at the assailant is essential in order to know exactly where he is positioned. Bend forward at the waist for good balance, while lifting the thigh of the kicking leg up into the chest (115).

• *Action*: Vigorously drive the leg straight back into the shin, knee or groin. Strike with the heel of the foot, and at impact the foot should be vertical with the heel up (116, 117). Practice with a pillow. Return to the starting position ready to repeat the kick or escape.

OTHER KICKS

If your assailant is very close and your body movement is restricted, there are several other kicking techniques that may be used effectively by women. Any one of these techniques may be sufficient for a release from a hold.

FOOT STOMP

This kick may be used against either a front or rear attack. Stomp the heel or the sole of the foot down vigorously on top of the instep of the opponent's foot. Repeat if necessary.

115. BACK KICK—STARTING POSITION

116. BACK KICK—
FINISH

117. BACK KICK—
PRACTICE WITH
PILLOW

KNEE-UP TO THE GROIN

Contrary to popular belief, this kick is not the best kick to use against a male attacker. Generally, men are prepared to defend themselves against this type of kick. However, if done accurately and with surprise, this kick can be most successful in stopping a male attacker. Do not attempt to knee-up to the groin unless very close to the opponent. Drive the knee-up vigorously into the groin, and if that is not effective, be prepared to do another knee-up, foot stomp or other close-type defensive attack. Be prepared to escape quickly, since if he is not incapacitated, your assailant is most likely to be enraged and go after you with even more intensity.

A knee-up to the face may also be used if the attacker is bent over to the front of the victim (118).

SHIN-SCRAPE-STOMP

This technique is used when the attacker is either to the front or rear. Turn the foot to the side and scrape down his shin, and then stomp vigorously onto the instep of his foot. Repeat if necessary.

Basic Kick Defense: Jump Back and Foot Block

Since the kick is relatively easy to use, even the most inexperienced attacker may attempt to kick a victim. It is important for a woman to be able to react quickly against a kicking attack.

JUMP BACK

The best defense against most types of kicks is to jump back out of the range of the kick. This defense may be used for almost any kick—slow or fast, high or low!

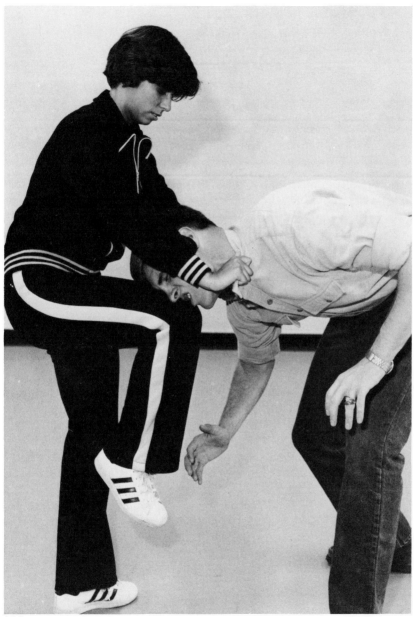

118. **KNEE-UP KICK TO FACE**

119. KICK DEFENSE—JUMP BACK

• *Starting Position*: From a defensive stance with
the knees bent, jump back with both legs as the
attacker starts the kick (before full leg extension).
Put as much distance between you and the attacker
as quickly as possible (119). Be ready to escape
or retaliate with a kick if the attacker immediately
comes after you again.

• *Practice*: If practicing alone, jump back as far
as possible from a stationary object—such as a
chair set in the middle of a room. If practicing
with a partner, have the kicker kick with a front or

side kick slowly at first, and react with a jump back. Gradually increase the speed of the kick and jump back.

FOOT BLOCK

If in a confined area (i.e., up against a wall) and there is no space and perhaps no time to jump back, a foot block may be used—especially against low kicks to the shin or knee. The block must be (120) done at the beginning of the kick before any full force can be behind it.

120. FOOT BLOCK DEFENSE AGAINST KICK

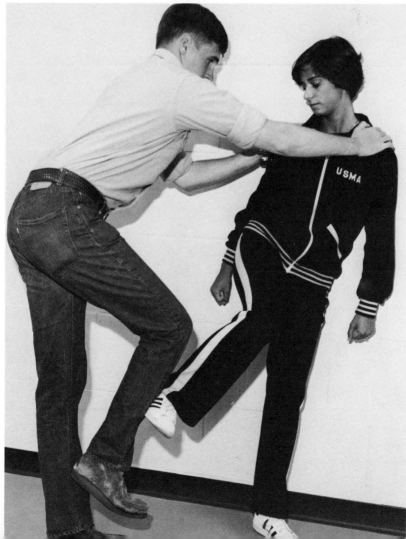

- *Starting Position*: From a defensive stance, shift your weight to the rear foot.
- *Action*: Lift the front leg and thrust out the side of the foot at the attacker's shin to stop the kick. Quickly return to the starting position ready to block again or retaliate with a kick.
- *Practice*: Have a partner wear a knee pad or other such padding on the shin for protection. Initially, kick in slow motion (front kick) and have the defender execute the foot block. Gradually increase the speed of the kick and block; never practice at full force since the shin on both individuals could be bruised.

6 Strikes and Strike Defenses

Basic Strikes

Generally, a woman should not try to defend herself against a male opponent by using only strikes and punches. Realistically, most women have neither the experience nor the necessary strength and power to get into a fistfight with a man. However, there is a basic punch, as well as several hand techniques, that, if properly practiced and learned, may be used as an integral part of self-defense. This chapter examines these techniques. Strike defenses will also be discussed in this chapter. Any woman who wants to defend herself properly should be prepared to try to ward off a slap or a punch by an assailant. Overcoming the shock of being struck may not be easy for some women. The fact remains, however, that in many attack situations, an assailant will attempt to strike or slap his victim.

GUIDELINES: Strikes, similar to kicks, should always be used against the vulnerable areas of the body. Since the woman's hand is normally not a firm, hard weapon, the bony or muscular areas of an assailant should not be struck (e.g., avoid striking his jaw or chest). Good targets include the eyes, nose, throat, groin and solar plexus (stomach area).

Strikes may be used as both distractions and retaliations. They should be executed quickly, accurately, with full force and with no hesitation or reservations. Angering an opponent with a poorly executed hand technique can easily result in a more determined and violent assault. Be confident. Maintain visual contact with your attacker. Do not look at the area to be struck. If your strike momentarily startles or hurts your assailant, be prepared to run or escape immediately.

BASIC PUNCH: If used properly the basic punch can be an excellent weapon for a woman. However, thrown incorrectly, the punch can result in an injury to an individual's knuckles, fingers, wrist or elbows. The primary body areas to attack with the basic punch are the nose, throat, solar plexus, floating ribs, groin and kidneys.

• *Starting Position*: From a basic defensive stance with the striking hand held in at the side of the body, make a secure fist with the palm up. Having the palm up is somewhat unconventional, but the reason will become clear in the action described below. Curl the fingers into a tight ball and wrap the thumb over the fingers. Do not put the thumb inside the fist or point it upward. A step may be taken with the punch, although it is not necessary (121).

• *Action*: Keep the fist tight and the wrist straight. The elbow should drive the fist forward. Just before contact, the wrist is half turned (palm turning inward), and the elbow is straightened. The striking surface is

121. BASIC PUNCH—
STARTING POSITION

122. BASIC PUNCH—
FINISH

123. BASIC PUNCH—PRACTICE FROM KNEELING POSITION

the largest two knuckles. At the same speed and force, the nonstriking arm is pulled in the opposite direction of the punch (122). This balances the punch and adds strength by putting the shoulder behind the force. Be careful not to throw the shoulders, lead with the elbow or bend the wrist at contact. Immediately withdraw the punch and return to the starting position. Be ready to strike again if necessary. At contact, the victim can shout or yell (e.g., "HIT!") to distract the assailant. In addition, shouting forcefully expels air from the lungs, enabling more force and power to be developed for the punch.

• *Practice*: From a kneeling position, punch out slowly, gradually increasing to full speed. Change the point of aim: straight forward (e.g., solar plexus); upward (e.g., throat); and downward (e.g., groin) (123).

From a standing position, punch at different speeds in all directions. Throw single right and left punches and then two or three punches in succession. Using an object, lean a chair or sofa cushion against a wall. At arm's distance from the object, punch from a kneeling position (124). If a partner assists, the cushion may be steadied or held up higher to allow practice from a standing position (125).

• *Note*: Be sure to practice punching with both the right and the left hand. Generally, the basic punch is easier to throw with the dominant, rather than the nondominant, hand. However, since a woman does not know from which direction she may be attacked, she must be prepared to strike with either hand.

KNIFE EDGE HAND STRIKE: This is one of the best hand techniques for a woman to use. It is powerful and requires little strength. It has less injury potential to the user since the more protected fleshy side of the

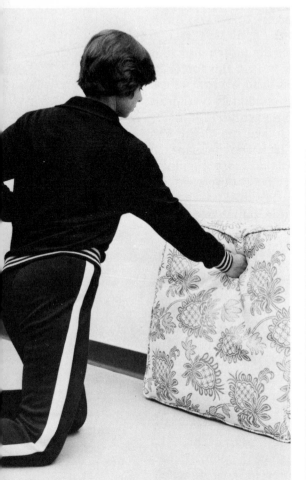

124. BASIC PUNCH—
PRACTICE FROM KNEELING
POSITION WITH PILLOW

125. BASIC PUNCH—
PRACTICE FROM STANDING
POSITION WITH PILLOW

hand—the part under the little finger—is the striking surface. The primary body areas to attack are the temple, nose (bridge), neck (sides), throat, clavicle, and groin.

• *Starting Position*: From a basic defensive stance, the striking hand should be held up near the head. The knife edge hand: The fingers are extended and joined with the thumb bent inward. The fingertips are just slightly bent while the hand is arched or bowed back. The knuckles are aligned and the wrist is straight.

• *Action*:

1. Bending the elbow, draw the knife edge hand to the opposite ear and strike out with a snap of the hand and extension of the elbow. At the same time pull the other arm back slightly to counter the forward momentum of the striking hand (126). A shout may be used at contact. Quickly return the arms to the starting position—ready to strike again if necessary.

2. With the elbow bent, draw the knife edge hand from the same ear and strike down with a snap of the hand and extension of the elbow. Keep the wrist straight (127).

• *Practice*: It is best to practice striking an object. From a kneeling position, an arm's distance from a cushion, strike, drawing from the opposite ear and contact the side of the target. Then strike drawing from the same ear and contact on top of the target (128).

From a standing position, with a partner securing or holding the target, repeat as above (129). Be sure that the partner secures the target and is out of the way of the strike. Practice with both a left and right knife edge hand.

126. KNIFE EDGE HAND
STRIKE—FROM OPPOSITE
EAR: STARTING POSITION

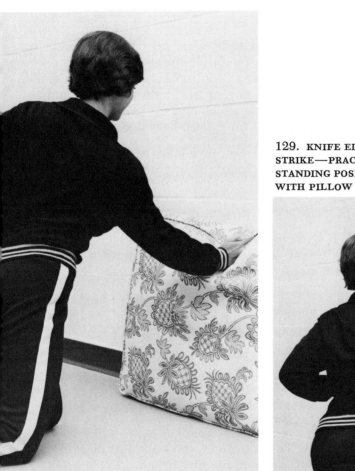

129. KNIFE EDGE HAND
STRIKE—PRACTICE FROM
STANDING POSITION
WITH PILLOW

128. KNIFE EDGE HAND
STRIKE—PRACTICE FROM
KNEELING POSITION
WITH PILLOW

Other Hand Techniques

Several other hand techniques may be used effectively by women for defending themselves. Since they're generally self-explanatory, only a brief description of them is presented. Many of the same principles and guidelines for the basic punch and the knife edge hand strike are also applied for these other hand techniques.

PINCH AND TWIST: Sensitive areas of the attacker's body: ears, nose, lip, inner thigh, groin, testicles, and armpit.

SCRATCH: Especially if your fingernails are long.

SPEAR HAND: With joined, extended fingers, jab at the eyes, throat, area above upper lip and gag reflex (bottom of throat).

THUMB GOUGE: To attack the eyes: Place fingers at side of the head, with thumbs in corners of eyes near nose—rake thumbs outward across eyes.

EXTENDED KNUCKLE PUNCH: With fingertips curled tightly and thumb tucked to side of hand, punch with extended knuckles at throat, above upper lip and back of attacker's hand.

ELBOW JAB: If attacked from the rear, strike back hard with bent elbow to the face (nose, lips or chin), the solar plexus and floating ribs, or down to the groin area.

STRIKE DEFENSE: The average male attacker may very probably attempt to strike the intended victim. Therefore, it is imperative that a woman be able to react quickly to protect herself against these strikes.

JUMP BACK: Since a punch is usually thrown quickly, the strike defense must also be fast. Since it is almost instinctive to jump back away from any attempted strike, these actions constitute the best and easiest defense to use. The basic principle here is simply to move out of the line of attack.

- *Starting Position*: Basic Defensive Stance.
- *Action*: Jump back as far away from the strike as possible. The front arm is kept up high with the forearm protecting the face and head area (130). Be ready to retaliate with a side snap kick to the knee, shin or groin while escaping, although if far enough away to escape, by all means, ESCAPE!!!
- *Practice*: If alone, practice jumping away from imaginary punches. With a partner, stand arm's distance apart. Start slowly by jumping away from your part-

130. **STRIKE DEFENSE—JUMP BACK**

ner's roundhouse-type punch (the most commonly used punch by an assailant). Then have your partner increase the speed of the punch and change to a jab or straight-on type punch without actually making contact. Also, be careful to have your partner aim the punches so you don't get hurt if you move too slowly. Practice defense against both left and right hand punches.

Step Back and Kick

If the punch is thrown quickly and forcefully, there may not be enough time for you to jump back. In that case, you should try to either step back or shift your body away from the punch. Since the victim is fairly close to the attacker, this should be immediately followed by a side snap kick to the attacker's groin, knee or shin (131).

• *Starting Position*: Basic defensive stance with one arm kept up high at all times to protect the head.

• *Action*: As the punch begins, duck the head and shoulders and step back or shift the body away from the attacker. Immediately kick as you continue to retreat. While stepping back may not totally prevent the punch from landing, it should lessen the impact and prevent the assailant from grabbing you.

• *Practice*: If alone, practice a step back and kick. With a partner, practice while using slow, roundhouse-type punches.

Forearm Block

Another strike defense that should be only used as a last resort is a double forearm block. If a high, over-

131. STRIKE DEFENSE—STEP BACK AND KICK

the-head-type punch is directed downward at the face
or head, and the defender is either confined or does not
have time to either jump back or step away, the strike
may be blocked by the forearm(s). This is dangerous

because it will probably result in severe bruising or even breakage of the forearm bones. It is discussed here since it may save the victim from a serious or fatal blow to the head.

In an effort to protect the bony part of the forearm, the block is made with the muscular or padded part of the arm (with the palms of the hands toward the face). The arms are held up in front of the face close to each other with the elbows nearly touching (132).

132. STRIKE DEFENSE—FOREARM BLOCK

7 Defense Against Frontal Attacks

Assailants use many different types of frontal attacks against women. The most common types of frontal holds and attacks are discussed in this chapter: wrist, shoulder, chokes, lapel, hair pull, rushes and hugs. Fortunately, every type of frontal hold and attack can be defended against by a number of techniques. In order to confine a discussion of these techniques to reasonable limits, only the best, most practical and proven defense methods are presented in this chapter. These techniques are easy to learn, and are almost instinctive reactions to frontal attack situations. A self-defense skill that is too complex either to learn, or to master completely, may easily lead to self-defeat rather than self-defense.

General Guidelines

The defender should move as quickly and effectively as possible to escape a frontal attack, no matter how minor it may seem to be. You should particularly try to escape a totally restrictive type of hold, such as a bear hug, which is much harder to break than a less confining type, such as a wrist hold.

Most of the defenses and releases for frontal holds include both a distraction and a retaliation. A distraction is used to help loosen an assailant's hold. In some instances, a distraction may also be effective enough by itself to result in the victim being released. A retaliation is used after the victim's release to discourage her assailant from regrabbing, or again attacking her. Typical distractions and retaliations include kicks and strikes to vulnerable parts of the body. If the distraction and release are successful to the degree that the victim moves safely out of reach of her assailant, a retaliation may not be advisable. Every woman should remember that the primary objective in a situation requiring self-defense is to *escape*, not inflict punishment upon her attacker.

The type of distraction, release and retaliation that should be used depends upon the seriousness of the attack situation. In a very small amount of time, the woman must decide if her life is being threatened and act accordingly. In reality, the self-defense techniques are dictated by both the attack situation and the defensible skills of the victim. For example, a woman might use either a knee-up to the groin or an eye gouge on a potential rapist, but would probably not employ similar techniques against a drunk at a party trying to put his arm around her shoulder! Remember self-defense may range from trying to talk an assailant out of the attack to scratching out his eyes.

Practicing the defenses and releases against frontal holds is extremely important. On the other hand, practice is quite different from a real attack situation. In practices with a friend or a partner, no element of surprise exists. The partner holding her knows exactly what she is going to do. In addition, the factor of pain is practically eliminated. It is doubtful, for example, that an individual will kick her husband or acquaintance in the shins while practicing a wrist release. Consequently, her partner must cooperate to the extent that if a simulated blow looks as though it would cause a release, then he should release the hold. The practice partner also needs to vary the degree of the holds, starting with half-strength and working up to full-strength holds. This should improve both the practice environment and the resultant learning. Another technique that can be employed to improve the practice situation is to increase the element of uncertainty by having the "victim" partner close her eyes and be attacked by her "assailant" partner. As soon as a hold is applied, her eyes should be opened and the appropriate defense techniques practiced.

Wrist Releases

While there are several types of wrist holds, this chapter examines those most commonly used by assailants: single or 1 on 1, double—2 on 1 and 2 on 2. Each wrist hold and the corresponding method(s) of defense for the hold are described. In a majority of the cases, the guidelines are identical for all the wrist releases.

GUIDELINES: Generally, the wrist hold is one of the easiest frontal holds from which to escape. It is less confining and threatening than most of the other holds. It also leaves several personal weapons free for counterattack.

As soon as the wrist is grabbed, a woman should initiate her defensive actions imm diately, before her assailant can apply his full force to the hold. As a rule, a woman should not try to *match* her strength against that of a man's. The chances of successfully pulling back and away from an assailant who is holding her wrist is very slight. The techniques presented in this chapter offer a much better defense. At all times, try to stay a safe distance from the holder to prevent him from getting a more secure hold. Keep that arm's distance between you and the attacker, if at all possible.

Single—1 on 1 (front hold over, under or side grip):

This is one of the most common of the wrist holds. An assailant reaches out to grab the wrist of a victim

133. FRONT WRIST 1 ON 1—HOLD

and attempts to pull her close to him (133). It is also one of the easiest to defend against, since only one wrist is being held. Be careful of the opponent's free hand, which may be used as a striking hand.

- *Starting Position*: Basic defensive stance.
- *Action*: Immediately distract—yell; stomp his instep with your heel; front or side kick the knee or shin. Such actions may be enough to secure your release, but if they are not, take a step around your assailant to pull him off balance momentarily. At the same time, shoot your elbow up toward him—holding your forearm very close to your upper arm. Turn the wrist being held and pull it up and away over your shoulder (134). Pull against the thumb and forefingers of the assailant

134. FRONT WRIST 1 ON 1—RELEASE

135. FRONT WRIST 1 ON 1—CLOSE UP OF WRIST TWIST OUT

since this is the weakest part of his grip (135). The release is like a crowbar. Quickly retaliate with a side kick to his knee as you escape.

• *Practice*: If alone, practice stepping, the release and the retaliation. With a partner, practice a distraction, release and retaliation. Vary the strength and the type of the hold—right, left, over, under, side, stationary and moving (grab and pull along). Practice with the eyes closed.

Double: 2 on 1

One wrist is held by both of the assailant's hands
(over, under, or side grip) (136). This is a more difficult wrist hold to escape since it is more restrictive and
involves a more forceful hold by the assailant. However, the victim does have the advantage that one of
her hands is free while both of the assailant's are
occupied.

• *Starting Position*: Basic defensive stance.

• *Action*: Immediately distract to help loosen the hold
(see 1 on 1). While stepping around and away from
the assailant, reach in with the free hand and grab
the top of the hand that is being held (137); pull it up
and away toward your opposite shoulder. (If you pull

136. FRONT WRIST 2 ON 1—HOLD

137. FRONT WRIST 2 ON 1—RELEASE, REACH AND GRAB HAND

over the shoulder of the arm being held, you may hit yourself in the face!) Use total body movement to pull free—bend the knees, use the shoulders, and step back all at once. Quickly, retaliate with side kick and escape (138).

• *Note*: If the wrist cannot be pulled free, continue with distractions and constant movement. A moving victim is harder to hold.

• *Practice*: If alone, practice distraction, release and retaliation. With a partner, practice with varying degrees of strength and types of holds—right, left, over, under and side grips. Practice stationary and moving with the eyes opened and closed.

138. **FRONT WRIST 2 ON 1—FINISH RELEASE AND RETALIATE**

Double: 2 on 2

Both wrists are held in front by the assailant (over or under grip).

While this is difficult to dislodge since it is both confining and forceful, it also places the assailant in a somewhat neutral, awkward position. Since the assail-

139. FRONT WRIST 2 ON 2—PULL ARMS
OUTWARD MOMENTARILY

ant is using both his hands to hold his victim, he has
to let go of something to assault his victim further.

- *Starting Position*: Basic defensive stance.
- *Action*: Immediately distract to loosen the hold (see
1 on 1). While stepping, momentarily swing the hands
outward (139) and then quickly pull them inward, up
and away (140) as with the 1 on 1 release. Retaliate
with front snap kick and escape.
- *Practice*: See 2 on 1 above.

140. **FRONT WRIST 2 ON 2—RELEASE AND KICK**

141. FRONT SHOULDER GRAB—STEP AND PUT ARM UP

Shoulder Grab Releases (front and side)

An assailant may grab onto both shoulders either to shake the victim, pull her in closer, or throw her to the ground. The defenses for this hold are relatively simple. The release should be done quickly, since this particular hold is usually a prelude to a more dangerous and restrictive-type hold. The defense approach should include a distraction (which may be enough for a release), a release and a retaliation while escaping. Be careful not to be regrabbed.

SHOULDER GRAB RELEASE (front)
- *Starting Position*: Basic defensive stance.
- *Action*: Quickly distract: yell; stomp instep; shin-scrape and stomp instep; kick knee or shin; or use a hand strike to the face. Step *back* away (147) and try to dislodge your assailant's hands from off your shoulders with a blow from your fist, swung hard in an arc from the outside in (this is a roundhouse punch). Use total body movement in punching up and across in front of your body (142, 143). Quickly retaliate and escape, e.g., elbow jab to face, or side kick to knee.
- *Practice*: If alone, practice a distraction, the step and punch, and a retaliation. With a partner, practice the distraction, release and retaliation. Have your partner use different degrees of force for the hold. Be careful to avoid actually hitting your partner with either the distraction or the retaliation. Practice with eyes opened and closed. Practice both situations—when you are grabbed only and when you are grabbed and shaken.

SHOULDER GRAB RELEASE (side): This may only be an annoyance-type hold where someone puts an arm around the shoulders. It could also be an attempt to pull the victim closer for a more confining hold.

142. **FRONT SHOULDER GRAB—RELEASE, ARM OVER PART I**

143. **FRONT SHOULDER GRAB—RELEASE, ARM OVER PART II**

- *Note*: This defense should also be used against a side-hug around the waist (147).
- *Starting Position*: Basic defensive stance.
- *Action*: Quickly distract: stomp on instep; elbow jab to groin (144); or turn in slightly and use a hand strike to the face. Aim for groin if it's a serious and threatening attack. If these are insufficient to effect a release, grab one or two of the assailant's fingers at the base and pull back and away (145). At the same time, step to the outside and behind the opponent (146). Retaliate as you escape with a side kick to knee.

144. SIDE SHOULDER HUG—DISTRACT
WITH HIT TO GROIN

145. SIDE SHOULDER HUG—RELEASE WITH FINGER PEEL

146. SIDE SHOULDER HUG—RELEASE FURTHER
WITH STEP OUT AND KICK

• *Practice*: This should be with a partner. Simulate the
blows for distraction. Practice the finger pull, being
careful not to bend your partner's fingers too far backward. Practice from both left and right sides, stationary
and moving (pulling along). Practice may be against

holds made either with the arm around the shoulder or around the waist.

Front Choke Release

This could be a 1 or 2 hand front choke. A choke is one of the most frightening and serious forms of

147. SIDE WAIST HUG—FINGER PEEL FOR RELEASE

frontal attacks. If held forcefully for an extended period of time, it may result in impaired breathing, unconsciousness, and even death. Unfortunately, it is frequently used against women.

GUIDELINES: Defensive actions against a choke should be implemented very quickly. The victim must not PANIC! Even if free breathing is impaired momentarily, if she employs the proper defensive actions, she will have enough time to escape. She should never grab at the hands of her assailant to try to peel his fingers off her throat. This attempt to match her strength with that of her opponent's will most likely be a waste of precious time. Since this is a life-or-death situation, the most serious and injurious types of defenses should be used without any hesitation whatsoever.

Practicing the choke release is essential to proper learning. Certain precautions, however, should be followed while practicing the choke release. When practicing these defenses with a partner, injuries can be avoided by not using a full force choke with the thumbs pressing into the throat. Rather, practice the chokes with the hands either low around the collarbone or with the thumbs along the sides of the neck (148). Also, just to be safe, have a nonverbal signal for your partner to release the hold if it is painful. For example, tap the floor with the foot twice, or tap the side of your thigh twice or tap the partner's arm twice, etc. The person who is applying the choke hold should be very alert to release the hold immediately if the partner taps out!

Since the choke is a hold applied in close proximity, be sure that the release puts you a safe enough distance from the attacker so that he cannot easily re-

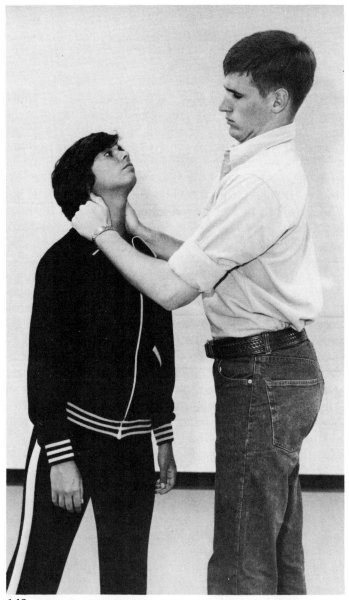

**148. TWO HANDS FRONT CHOKE—THUMBS AT SIDES
OF NECK FOR SAFETY IN PRACTICE**

choke or regrab you. In addition, your retaliation should be vicious enough that the assailant will be discouraged from continuing his attack against you.

Front Choke Release—1 Hand

With one hand an assailant may grab his victim by the throat, pushing her back into a corner or up against a wall for further attack (149). Be careful of the assailant's free hand, which may be used to strike.
• *Starting Position*: Basic defensive stance.
• *Action*: As the assailant grabs at the throat, first try to duck, avoid, and step away. If grabbed, quickly distract: stomp instep; kick knee or shin; knee groin; attack face and gouge eyes; etc. If not released, quickly

149. ONE HAND FRONT CHOKE, AGAINST WALL—HOLD

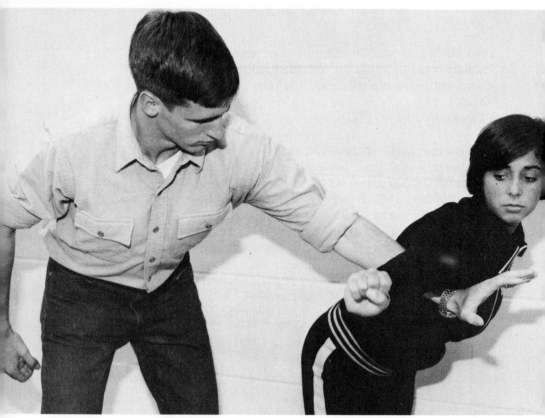

150. ONE HAND FRONT CHOKE, AGAINST WALL—RELEASE, ARM UP AND OVER

step *forward* and laterally, and do a roundhouse punch across the body (150). (See the preceding Front Shoulder Grab Release.) Immediately, retaliate if you can do so keeping a safe distance away, while escaping. Throughout the defense, be ready to protect against a strike to your head by the assailant's free hand.

• *Practice*: If alone, practice a distraction, the step and punch, and a retaliation. With a partner, practice a distraction, release and retaliation from a right- and left-hand stationary, and moving (pushing) choke. Remember to practice the choke hold at the collarbone or with the thumbs along the side of the neck for safety reasons.

Front Choke Releases—2 Hands

This is a much stronger and more dangerous choke hold. The defenses must be immediate, before either panic or unconsciousness occur. While there are several defense techniques for this type of hold, only the two best releases are described in this section.

- *Starting Position*: Basic Defensive Stance.
- *Action*: As the assailant grabs at your throat with both hands, first try to duck, avoid, and step away. If grabbed and choked, use a quick and painful distraction, e.g., gouge eyes; knee-up to groin; or strike throat and employ gag reflex. To release: (1) Use same technique as with front shoulder grab release, or (2) wedge-up—with knees and elbows bent, clasp hands together (do not interlace fingers) and hold low and close to the body (151); immediately straighten arms and legs, exploding hands (forming a wedge) up through assailant's arms (152). Retaliate with both hands hitting down on bridge of nose or clavicle; then escape (153). The wedge-up is not likely to be very effective, if the assailant is much taller and stronger than you.
- *Practice*: If alone, practice a distraction, both releases and a retaliation. With a partner, practice a distraction, releases and a retaliation from a stationary choke. Also, practice the choking situation against a wall (154, 155) both with the eyes opened and closed. Employ safety precautions with this choke. Do not choke with full force!

151. FRONT TWO HAND CHOKE, WEDGE-UP RELEASE—
STARTING POSITION

**152. FRONT TWO HAND CHOKE, WEDGE-UP—
FINISH**

153. **FRONT TWO HAND CHOKE—RETALIATION WITH HIT TO NOSE**

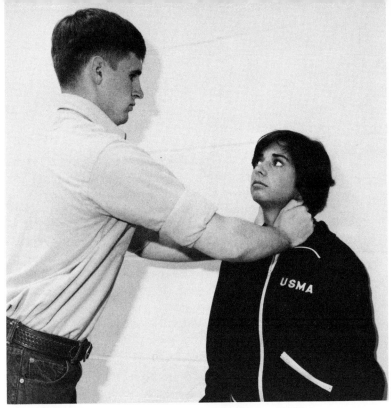

154. **FRONT TWO HAND CHOKE AGAINST WALL—HOLD**

155. **FRONT TWO HAND CHOKE AGAINST WALL—
RELEASE WITH ARM UP AND OVER**

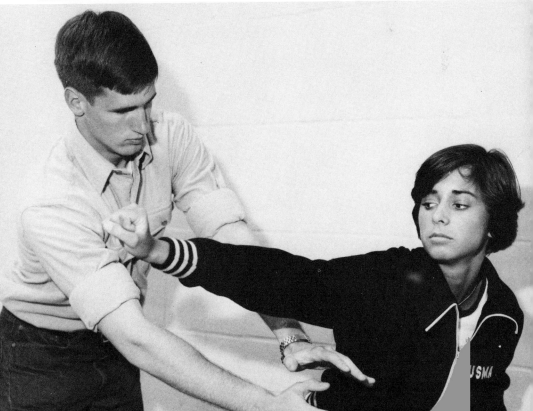

Lapel or Collar Grab Releases

This may be a single or double lapel or collar grab. The attacker may grab his victim by the clothing either to pull her in closer or to push her up against a wall for further attack. While this is not an attack commonly used against a woman, it is occasionally employed. The defense should be applied quickly, before a more forceful hold is applied. The best defense is to first try to avoid or step away from the attacker, as he reaches to grab the clothing. However, if grabbed, the defensive action should be the same as for a 2 hand front choke release—distract, release and retaliate. The best release is with the step and roundhouse punch (156).

156. DOUBLE LAPEL RELEASE—ARM UP AND OVER

Rushing Attack Defense

An attacker may attempt to rush his victim either to catch her, as for robbery or purse-snatching, or knock her down for further attack. The rush may be aimed low at the knees and legs, or high at the shoulders and head.

Your best defense is to go into action. As soon as a victim sees an assailant running at her, she should step out of the way and run to safety. The victim should also shout to startle the rusher and stall his attack. If these initial attempts fail to deter the rusher, the victim must employ additional defensive measures. Never try to oppose or block the momentum of the attacker's rush. Rather, go with his momentum. As the rusher reaches you, grab onto him and pull him by, either onto the ground or into an object such as a wall. Continue to counterattack with kicks and strikes, while he is down, and then escape.

The victim has the advantage of being able to step out of the way of the rushing assailant at the last minute. Once the attacker is on a full rush, it is usually quite difficult for him to change the direction of his attack.

Front Hair Pull Release

An assailant may attempt to grab or pull his victim's hair either to hurt her or to pull her in closer for further attack. This is a very painful attack, and should be repelled quickly.

• *Starting Position*: Basic defensive stance.

• *Action*: As the assailant grabs at the hair, first try to duck, avoid and step out of the way. If grabbed, quickly distract to lessen the hold: stomp instep; or kick knee or shin. Also, at the same time, clasp both hands down on top of assailant's hands above his wrist (157). Do not interlace your fingers. Keep your elbows in close to your body. This should help to relieve the pain of the hair pull. Then, immediately step back on one leg and curl head and chest forward and downward, pivoting around halfway, as curling (158). This movement should bend and twist the opponent's wrist uncomfortably and result in your release. Quickly, retaliate with a side kick and escape.

• *Practice*: Should be with a partner. Be careful that the partner does not grab too tightly, or actually pull

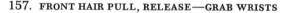

157. **FRONT HAIR PULL, RELEASE—GRAB WRISTS**

158. FRONT HAIR PULL, RELEASE—COME UP AND TWIST

a large amount of hair. Practice the distraction, release and retaliation. Also, be careful to do the release slowly, so that the holder's wrist is not forcefully hyperextended. Practice with both a right- and left-hand front hair pull. Practice only stationary, with the eyes open.

Front Hug Releases

This may be a body or bear hug from the front, either under or over the arms. Either way, it is one of the most confining and restrictive holds that an opponent can use against a woman from a standing position. It is usually a momentary hold to gain control of the victim, prior to throwing her to the ground for further attack. As such, it is a common attack and an extremely dangerous hold. It should be released as quickly as possible.

• *GUIDELINES*: There are several distractions or reactions that may be used effectively in succession against a front hug. Because the assailant is very close to his victim, he has many vulnerable body areas that are open to counterattack. The victim should select the distractions that work best for her, and use them. Also, as long as the front hug is being held, the assailant cannot attack further. In most instances, this will permit the victim more time to counterattack and hopefully escape.

As soon as the hug is applied, place the feet shoulder width apart, bend the knees and lower your center of gravity. This makes you a more difficult object to control, lift up and throw down to the ground. If there is a chance of your losing your balance and falling, try not to fall backwards where the assailant can land on top of you on the ground. Lean forward and try to fall, landing on top of the opponent—a position from which it is easier to defend yourself.

Since the hug is an extremely close attack, be sure that the release puts you a safe distance from your attacker. Discourage further attack, by using serious and painful types of distractions and retaliations.

Front Hug Release—Over the Arms

A front hug where the arms are pinned to the sides of the body is the most common type of front hug.

- *Starting Position*: Basic defensive stance.
- *Action*: As the attacker reaches to hug, first try to avoid or step away. If grabbed, quickly distract using three or four attacks in succession: yell; stomp instep; shin-scrape and stomp instep; kick knee or shin; knee to groin; clasp hands together if possible and punch groin (159); or butt forehead to face. Try to create space so the hold is not so confining. If the distractions do not result in a release, try jumping

159. FRONT HUG OVER ARMS—CREATE SPACE
WITH GROIN HIT

160. FRONT HUG OVER ARMS—RELEASE WITH JUMP DOWN AND BACK

downward and back away as the arms are lifted upward—like an umbrella (160). This should knock the
opponent's arms off your shoulders and upper arms.
If necessary, use your hands to help push his arms off
of you. Immediately retaliate as you escape and then
move a safe distance from the opponent.

• *Practice*: The jump may be practiced as described
above. With a partner, practice a series of distractions,
the release and a retaliation. Although the distractions
should not be applied full force, the hold should be
released once it appears as if the distractions would be
effective. Practice with different degrees of force in
holding, both with the eyes opened and closed. Practice
both stationary and moving.

Front Hug Release—Under the Arms

A front hug where both of the victim's arms are free
is an easier hug from which to escape because the
victim's hands and arms may be used in her release.
Although in most instances the attacker would usually
not grab under the arms, it might happen. It may also
be that the attacker did a front hug over the arms and
the victim was able to pull one or both arms free.

• *Starting Position*: Basic defensive stance.

• *Action*: Try first to avoid or step away, but, if grabbed,
use any three or four of the following distractions, as
quickly as possible: yell; attack the eyes; pinch and
twist the lip; punch the temples; strike the nose or
throat; knee the groin; use the gag reflex; kick and
scrape shins and stomp instep; or use the mastoid
process lift (see photo 26). Any combination of these
attacks should result in a release. Retaliate, while
escaping, and move a safe distance from the assailant.

- *Variation*: If you are hugged and immediately lifted up off the ground, try to hook a foot or ankle around the opponent's lower leg. He will be working against his own body weight as well as trying to lift your weight. Continue with distractions.
- *Practice*: Must be with a partner. Practice any of the distractions, being careful to simulate some blows and not using full force. Vary the force of the hug, and practice with eyes opened and closed. Practice both stationary and moving hugs.

8 Defense Against Attacks from the Rear

Although there are several types of attacks from the rear that may be used against a woman, only those most frequently used by assailants are discussed in this chapter: wrist, chokes, hair pull, hugs, double elbow lock, and 1 arm hammerlock. The defensive techniques and releases presented for each rear hold are simple, practical and proven.

• *General Guidelines*: Any kind of attack from the rear is a highly dangerous and frightening type of hold. Most attacks from the rear are a complete surprise to the victim, which makes defending against these attacks more difficult. The reaction to the attack must be immediate. In short, the defense techniques must be so well known by the victim that they are virtually instinctive. Any delay in the self-defense reaction may mean the difference between life and death.

Distractions and retaliations are a very important part of the defenses against attacks from the rear. In most instances, quick and accurate counterattacks to the assailant's vulnerable areas can enable a victim to

173

secure her release. These counters should usually be a series of three to four simultaneous blows. Since the chances are that a victim will not see her assailant, any attack from the rear should be, as a general rule, treated as an extremely dangerous and life-threatening act or assault and her counters should be forceful ones.

Similar to the frontal attack defenses, practicing the defenses for the attack from the rear is vital if a woman wants to learn the proper techniques and to be able to execute these techniques quickly and accurately. Partners need to cooperate and to observe safety precautions at all times. Be very careful while practicing the rear chokes. Full force should not be used while practicing these holds. In addition, simulated counterattacks should be used, rather than making actual contact. In order to simulate more closely the surprise element of an attack from the rear, the "defender" partner should close her eyes while practicing her defensive reactions and techniques.

Rear Wrist Release—2 on 2

One type of assault from the rear occurs when both wrists are grabbed from behind and held by an assailant. His grip may be either overhand or underhand. The aim of his attack may be to control the victim, to pull her closer to him or to pull her to the ground for further attack. Although this hold places a woman in a somewhat awkward position, it is easier to escape it than from a more confining hold, such as the rear hug. Consequently, the release can be quick. The victim should be careful to stay a safe distance from the attacker once she is released. A common error made while trying to escape from this hold is the victim's attempt to step forward and pull the arms straight out of the hold. This is usually a waste of time and energy since the assailant is frequently stronger than the victim.

• *Starting Position*: Basic defensive stance with backward position to the attacker.

• *Action*: As soon as the wrists are grabbed, distract to the rear: yell; back kick to the knee or shin; stomp the instep; or scrape the shin and then stomp the instep. Momentarily step back toward the attacker with knees bent and body leaning forward (161); then quickly step forward with the elbows bent in close to the sides of the body and then pull the wrists forward, up and away as with a single wrist release (162). Retaliate with a side snap kick to the knee while escaping. Do not step back toward the attacker to kick him. Kick only from a safe distance while you are stepping away.

• *Note*: The initial step back toward the assailant is immediate and should be performed in conjunction with the distraction. Hopefully, this backward move will momentarily confuse the assailant, who is probably expecting his victim to attempt to escape by pulling forward.

• *Practice*: If alone, practice the step back and the distraction, then the forward release. Timing is important. With a partner, practice the distraction, release and retaliation. Vary the degree of force in applying the hold. Practice with the eyes both opened and closed. Practice with both a stationary and moving hold.

Rear Choke Releases

This may be a 1 hand, 2 hand or forearm choke from behind. As with front chokes, the possibility of impaired breathing, unconsciousness and even death ex-

**SELF-DEFENSE
FOR WOMEN**

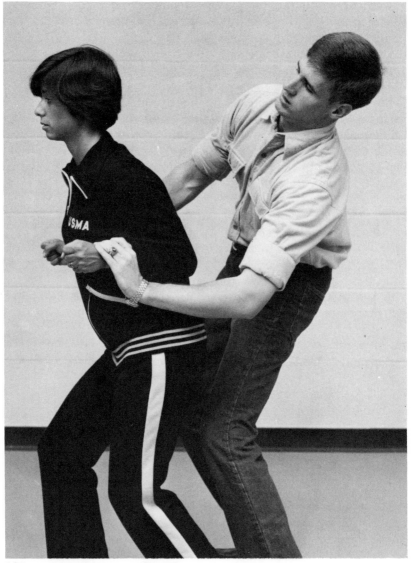

161. REAR WRIST HOLD, 2 ON 2—
START RELEASE WITH STEP BACK

162. REAR WRIST HOLD, 2 ON 2—
FINISH RELEASE WITH STEP AWAY

ists with any of these rear chokes. Unfortunately these
very dangerous holds are frequently used in assaults
on women. They must be reacted to with speed and
efficiency. It is no time to panic! In these life-or-death-
type holds, use only the most vicious distractions and
retaliations. Practice is essential, but be careful that
full force while choking is not used. Simulate your
counterattack while observing all safety precautions.
Employ the same "modified" choke and "tap-out"
method as was used to practice frontal chokes in
Chapter 7.

1 HAND OVER MOUTH RELEASE: This hold is typically used by an assailant to keep his victim quiet while
he attempts to gain control for a more serious type of
attack. In this type of hold, one hand usually covers the
victim's mouth very tightly while the other grabs her
arm or upper body pulling her closer to the assailant.
Since her breathing may be impaired, the victim must
secure a release quickly.

• *Starting Position*: Basic defensive stance with backward position to the attacker.

• *Action*: Distract immediately: try to bite the hand;
yell; back kick the knee or shin; stomp the instep; elbow
jab the solar plexus; or punch the groin. If still held,
reach up and grab 1 or 2 fingers (163) (little finger is
often the weakest) and pull back and away. Step off
to the side of the attacker while pulling at his fingers.
Retaliate with a side snap kick to the side of the knee
as escaping. Be sure to stay a safe distance from the
assailant once released.

• *Practice*: Must be with a partner. Practice a distraction, the release and retaliation. Be careful that the
partner's finger is not pulled too far back. Grab from
both sides of the defender. Practice with the eyes both

opened and closed. Practice both stationary and moving holds.

REAR CHOKE RELEASE—TWO HANDS: On this choke, the assailant has both his hands firmly around the neck of his victim from behind the victim. It is a very strong and frightening hold. Impaired breathing and unconsciousness may result within seconds. The release must begin the absolute second the choke is applied.

163. **REAR HAND OVER MOUTH HOLD—
RELEASE WITH FINGER PEEL**

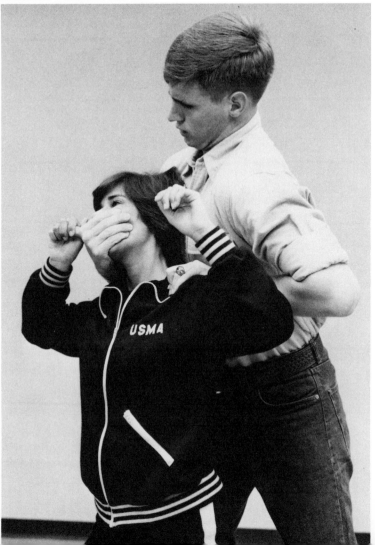

- *Starting Position*: Basic defensive stance with backward position to the attacker.
- *Action*: The distraction is optional. The victim may want to go immediately into the release. If, however, the release is not totally effective, then distractions should be used immediately. (See preceding 1 Hand Over Mouth Release.) To release, quickly throw one arm up

164. TWO HAND REAR CHOKE—RELEASE
WITH ARM UP AND START TURN

stepping slightly forward and turning around to face the attacker (164). Turn in the same direction as the arm that is raised. The turn should knock the assailant's hands off the throat (165). Immediately retaliate with a strike down to the attacker's face or clavicle as you back away. Keep a safe distance from the assailant to avoid being choked again. Remember, as stepping

165. TWO HAND REAR CHOKE—FINISH RELEASE WITH FULL TURN OUT

away, the side of your body and not your back should be to the attacker. Do not turn your back on the attacker too quickly once you attempt to escape.

• *Practice*: If alone, practice the arm-up-and-turn and a retaliation. With a partner, practice all steps with your eyes both opened and closed. Do not use full force in choking. Follow all rules of safety. Practice only a stationary hold.

REAR FOREARM CHOKE RELEASE: This choke is applied from behind the victim with a forearm held firmly across her throat. The hold is usually the most dangerous of the choke holds because it is both strong and very confining. Unconsciousness may result within seconds. As soon as breathing is impaired, the victim may get some relief by turning her head into the crook of the attacker's elbow (166). The release should then

166. **REAR FOREARM CHOKE—TURN INTO CROOK OF ELBOW FOR RELIEF**

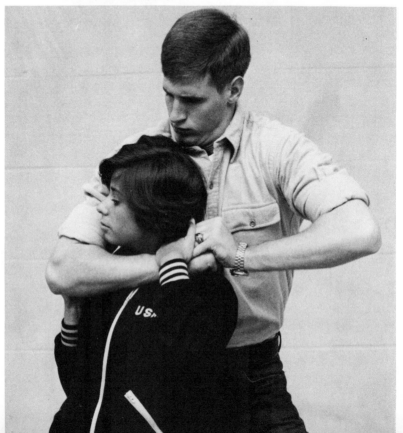

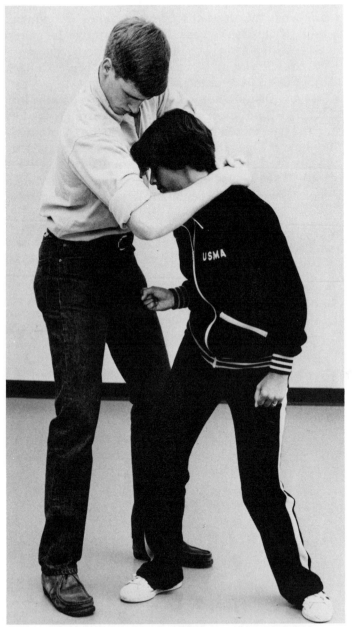

167. **REAR FOREARM CHOKE—RELEASE WITH TURN-IN
AND HIT GROIN**

follow. There is a possibility that the victim may either see or sense the attacker's arm as it comes around from behind. If this is the case, the victim might be able to duck and step away in time to avoid the choke.

• *Starting Position*: Basic defensive stance with backward position to the attacker.

• *Action*: Distract immediately to try to loosen the hold and create some space in which to move: yell; back kick shin or knee; punch the groin; elbow to the solar plexus; bite the arm; butt the head backwards to the attacker's head; or stomp the instep. There are two releases: (1) Turn-in: Swing the arm and shoulder (on the same side as is being held) down and around while stepping

168. REAR FOREARM CHOKE—RELEASE WITH COUNTER JOINT ACTION, CREATE SPACE

around to face the opponent (167). Quickly strike the
face or groin while backing away to safety. If the hold
is very strong, this release may not be effective. Speed
is very important. (2) Counter Joint Action: Place the
palm of one hand under the attacker's wrist, with the
fingers curling up under his lower arm, and the palm of
the other hand under his elbow joint. Simultaneously
pull down on the wrist and jerk up on the elbow creat-
ing a space (168). Turn the head inward and step
back, slipping down and out through the open space
(169). Be sure to step out backwards—do not turn
around to face the attacker. Quickly retaliate, such as
with a side snap kick to the side of the knee while

169. REAR FOREARM CHOKE—COUNTER JOINT RELEASE,
STEP BACK

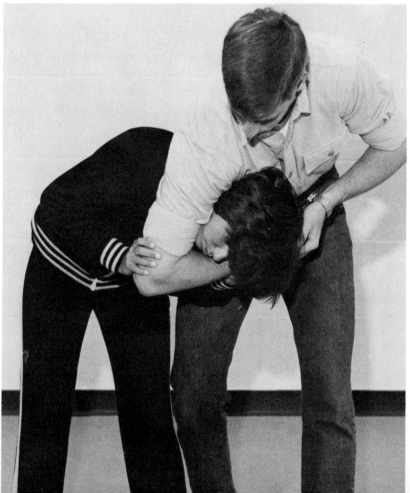

170. REAR FOREARM CHOKE—EXAMPLE OF HEAD LOCK AND
RESULTING GROIN HIT

escaping. If when trying to back out, the attacker gets your head into a headlock, viciously attack the groin, jab the eyes, stomp the instep, etc., until the release is completed (170).

• *Note*: Another release for this hold is a shoulder throw. It is not discussed in this text because throws generally are more difficult to learn, and they are not as practical as the aforementioned techniques. In addition, in order to practice the throws, a partner must be willing to be thrown and must know how to fall correctly in order to avoid possible injury.

• *Practice*: If alone, practice the release for the turn-in. The counter joint action must be practiced with a partner. Practice the releases initially in slow motion and then at a faster rate in order to achieve a realistic practice situation. Practice all safety precautions, especially the nonverbal "tap-out." Vary the force of the holds, choke from both sides of the victim. Practice with the eyes both opened and closed, and from a stationary as well as moving hold.

Rear Hair Pull

The victim's hair is grabbed from behind to off-balance her or gain control of her for further attack. Since this is a very painful hold, a release must be secured immediately.

• *Starting Position*: Basic defensive stance with backward position to the attacker.

• *Action*: A distraction is optional because the attacker may not be near enough to contact with blows. To release, immediately clasp both hands down hard on the assailant's wrist (171). This should help to relieve the pain of the pull. Bend the head and upper body slightly forward, while turning around abruptly to face your attacker. Quickly stand upright and even up on the toes to bend the attacker's wrist backwards (172). Retaliate with a front kick to the knee, shin or groin as you escape.

• *Practice*: Should be with a partner. Practice the release and retaliation. Be careful not to pull the hair too hard or bend the wrist too abruptly. Practice slowly and with the eyes open. Practice the grab from both sides of the defender. For safety, use only a stationary-type hair pull.

171. **REAR HAIR PULL—START RELEASE
BY GRASPING WRISTS**

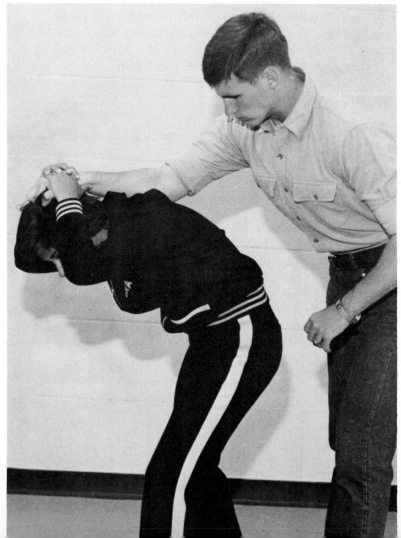

**172. REAR HAIR PULL—CONTINUE RELEASE BY TURNING
AND COMING UP**

Rear Hug Release

The victim may be held in a rear hug, over or under her arms (173). This is a more common type of hug attack than the front hugs. It is a confining, forceful hold. The rear hug may be applied by an assailant to control his victim, lift her up and throw her to the ground. Defenses should be quick and forceful. Since this type of hold may lead to a much more serious attack (e.g., rape), the distractions and retaliations

173. **REAR HUG OVER ARMS—HOLD**

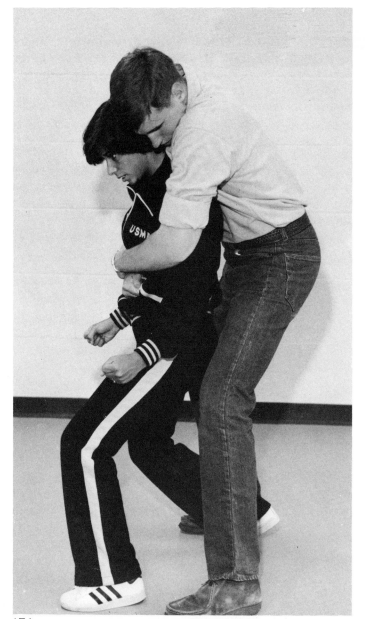

174. **REAR HUG OVER ARMS—START RELEASE BY LOWERING
CENTER OF GRAVITY**

should be extremely vicious. To be most effective, the distractions should be in a series of three or four as was described for defense against front hugs (Chapter 7, end). When grabbed, quickly try to bend the knees and lower the center of gravity (174). This should make it more difficult for the assailant to pick up his victim and throw her to the ground.

Rear Hug Release—Over the Arms

This type of rear hug occurs when the victim's arms are held tightly and are pinned to the sides of her body. This is the most common and dangerous type of rear hug attack.

• *Starting Position*: Basic defensive stance with backward position to the assailant.

• *Action*: As the attacker starts to grab you, try to step away and avoid before he can fully apply the hug. If grabbed, quickly distract, using three or four attacks in succession: e.g., yell; create space by moving the hips to one side and attacking the groin (175); kick back to the knee or shin; scrape the shin and stomp the instep; or butt the head back to the face. If still being held, try to grab one or two fingers and peel backwards while stepping away (176). If the hug is applied high on your arms, try to jump down and away as the arms are lifted abruptly upward (177). If the hug is low on the arms, escaping is more difficult. Step forward, at the same time twist the upper body and roll to the ground, falling across the shoulders onto your back. Land on top of the assailant if he continues to hold you (178). The momentum of the fall should loosen his hold. Immediately attack the face or groin and stand up to escape (179). Be sure to fall across your back— do not just step and fall forward or the assailant will

175. REAR HUG OVER ARMS—MOVE HIPS TO SIDE
AND HIT GROIN

176. **REAR HUG OVER ARMS—RELEASE WITH FINGER PEEL**

**177. REAR HUG OVER ARMS—RELEASE BY JUMPING
DOWN AND OUT**

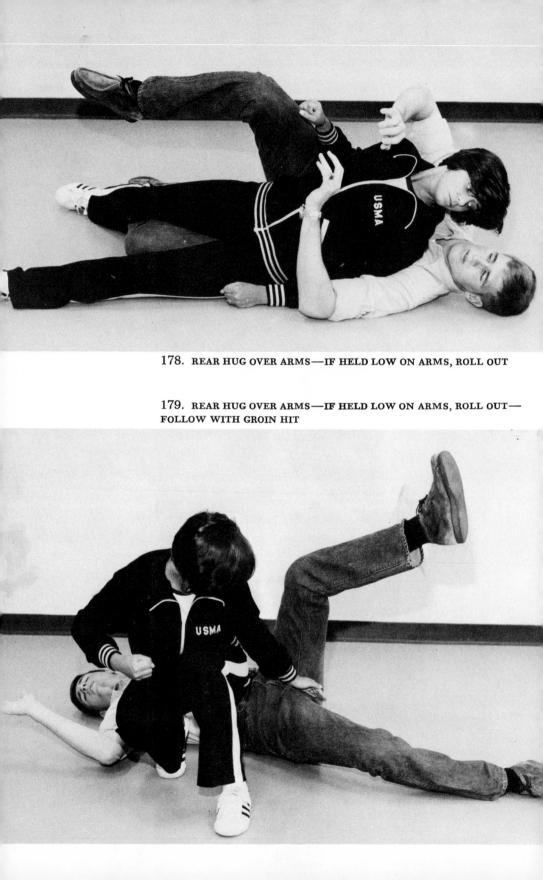

178. **REAR HUG OVER ARMS—IF HELD LOW ON ARMS, ROLL OUT**

179. **REAR HUG OVER ARMS—IF HELD LOW ON ARMS, ROLL OUT—FOLLOW WITH GROIN HIT**

fall on top of you! Retaliate after any of these releases with a side kick to the knee while escaping. Get a safe distance from the assailant to avoid being regrabbed. *Note*: Only use the roll to the ground as a last resort. The other escapes are safer. You do not want to go to the ground with the assailant unless absolutely necessary.

• *Note*: If an attacker grabs you and lifts you off the ground, try to hook his ankle or leg as he lifts you up (180). Continue with distractions. A moving and fighting victim is much harder to hold!

180. REAR HUG OVER ARMS—IF LIFTED UP, HOOK LEG

• *Practice*: If alone, practice the jump down and the roll out. With a partner, practice the distractions and each of the releases. Simulate blows and have the holder release accordingly. Vary the force of the hugs. Practice with the eyes both opened and closed, from a stationary and a moving hold. Also practice with the victim being lifted up.

Rear Hug—Under the Arms

This is a rear hug where both of the victim's arms are free. It is not as frequently used by assailants as the rear hug over the arms. It should be easier to escape from, since the arms, hands, and legs are free to counterattack.

• *Starting Position*: Basic defensive stance with backward position to the assailant.

• *Action*: As the attacker starts to hug you, try to avoid his hold. If grabbed, quickly execute three or four distractions in rapid succession: e.g., yell; reach back to grab his hair and pull his head forward to gouge his eyes (181); kick back to the shin or knee; shin-scrape and stomp instep; butt the head back to the face; or elbow jab back to the solar plexus and up to the face. If still held, knuckle punch the back of the hand, grab one or two fingers, peel back, and step out and away (182). A jump down or roll will not be an effective defensive action here. Once released, retaliate with a side kick to the knee as you escape.

• *Practice*: Must be with a partner. Practice a series of distractions, the finger peel and retaliation. Vary the force of the hold, practice with the eyes both opened and closed, and from a stationary and moving hug. Also practice the lift up.

**181. REAR HUG UNDER ARMS—
GRAB HAIR AND JAB EYES**

**182. REAR HUG UNDER ARMS—
RELEASE WITH FINGER PEEL**

Double Elbow Lock Release

The victim is grabbed from behind, with her elbows either locked or squeezed together. An attacker may control his victim in this manner prior to moving her to another place for further attack. Although it is a confining hold, it usually is not very painful. The victim has full use of the lower body to aid in her own self-defense.

• *Starting Position*: Basic defensive stance with backward position to the attacker.
• *Action*: Quickly distract to the rear: e.g., back kick to shin or knee; shin-scrape and stomp instep; or butt the head back into his face. Bend the body forward (183) and vigorously step forward, pulling both arms straight out of the hold (184). Retaliate with a side snap kick to the knee while you escape. Try to initiate

183. **REAR DOUBLE ELBOW HOLD—START RELEASE WITH BENDING AND STEPPING**

184. REAR DOUBLE ELBOW HOLD—FINISH RELEASE
BY PULLING ARMS STRAIGHT AWAY

the release as soon as he applies his hold, before the
hold can be executed with full force.

• *Practice*: Should be with a partner. Practice a distraction, the release and retaliation. Vary the force of
the hold, practice with the eyes both opened and closed,
and practice stationary and moving.

1 Arm Hammerlock Release

One arm is bent and pushed up the back. The victim's arm is usually held by an assailant at her wrist
and elbow to reinforce his hold and prevent her escape

(185). This may be used as a come-along hold to move a victim to another place. It is not a very secure hold and usually not too painful because most women have a wide range of flexibility in the shoulder joint. Also, the other arm and the legs are free to use in counter-attacking.

• *Starting Position*: Basic defensive stance with backward position to the attacker.

185. 1 ARM HAMMERLOCK—HOLD

• *Action*: Distract to the rear: e.g., with the free arm, strike the groin; elbow jab back to the solar plexus or up to the face; back kick to the knee or shin; or do a shin-scrape-stomp to the instep. If still held, step off to the side of the attacker, pulling your held arm straight out while stepping (186). Step to the same side as the arm being held. Execute a single wrist release (Chapter 7) if your wrist is still held (187).

186. 1 ARM HAMMERLOCK—START RELEASE BY WALKING OUT

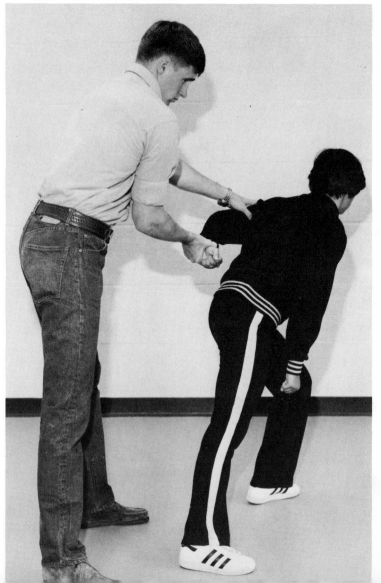

Quickly retaliate with a side snap kick to the side of the knee while you escape.

• *Practice*: Should be with a partner. Practice a distraction, the release and retaliation. Vary the force of the hold. Grab from both sides of the defender. Practice with the eyes both opened and closed, and from a stationary and moving hold.

187. 1 ARM HAMMERLOCK—FINISH RELEASE WITH WALK OUT AND THEN WRIST RELEASE

9 Defense Against a Weapon:
CLUB, KNIFE AND PISTOL

Always cooperate with an armed assailant. If his motive is robbery, give up your valuables. A general rule is never resist if a weapon is held directly to your body. However, as soon as the weapon is away from the body—react quickly and viciously. Remember, an armed assailant may only be using a weapon to threaten or frighten you into doing what he wants. As much as possible do as he says and save your life!

Since the possibility always exists that the armed assailant will attempt to kill his victim after robbing or assaulting her, defenses against weapon attacks should be learned. These should only be used as a *last resort*, as in a life-or-death situation. Weapon defenses presented in this chapter are for use against the most frequently carried weapons: a club, knife and pistol.

Club

A club can take many forms: a piece of wood, a lead pipe, a baseball bat, a broom handle, etc. The most

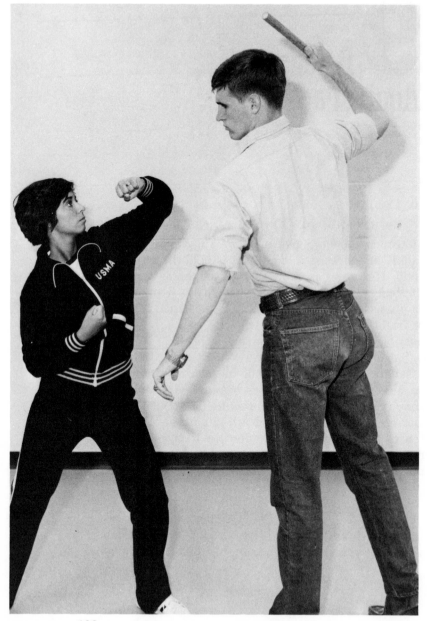

188. OVERHEAD CLUB ATTACK—HOLD

typical types of club attacks are striking from an overhead position downward toward the head; and striking from a sideward position hitting the neck or side of the body in the area of the kidneys or ribs. The defense is as follows:

• *Starting Position*: Basic defensive stance. This is very important because it places the side of your body to the attacker. This will give him fewer vulnerable areas to strike.

• *Action*: As soon as the strike begins (188), jump back as far as possible off both feet. One arm should be held up to protect the head (189). Try to hold the head off to one side for further protection. Quickly retaliate with a side snap kick to the knee or shin while escaping. Do not step back into the range of the club to kick your assailant. Keep a safe distance from his weapon.

189. OVERHEAD CLUB ATTACK—JUMP BACK

• *Note*: It is not recommended that the victim try to
block the club attack with her forearms. This could
result in serious injury. However, if you are in a confined space where jumping back is impossible, a last
resort would be to protect the head with the arms as
in the basic forearm block already presented in Chapter
6.

• *Practice*: This must be with a partner. Use a plastic
bat such as a Wiffle bat, or a cardboard tube, e.g., the
insert from a roll of wrapping paper. Practice swinging
the club from both overhead and sideways. Start with

190. **HOW TO USE A CLUB AGAINST ASSAILANT**

a slow swing and gradually increase to a more realistic type of attack. Practice the jump back and kick. Timing is most important.

HOW TO USE A CLUB: If the assailant drops the club or you happen in any way to gain possession of his weapon, use it with care. Do not swing the club. Hold it firmly in both hands and jab forward at vulnerable parts of the assailant's body, e.g., eyes, throat, or groin (190).

Knife

If at all possible, stay a safe distance from an attacker who has a knife. To use it, he must be close to you. If you are grabbed and the knife is held directly to your body, do not resist or move a muscle! Remain calm and try to talk to the assailant. Watch to see if the knife is put aside and then react! If the attack is an overhead or sideward thrust to your body, you have an opportunity to defend yourself. This is an instance where some defense is better than none since you probably will be seriously injured if you do nothing. Although you should expect to be cut while defending against a knife, being cut on the arm or leg is much better than being cut on the head or face area. Probably your only opportunity for defense will occur on the initial thrust. Be alert and quick to escape. Try to wrap a piece of clothing around one arm to aid in the defense. For an overhead or sideward knife thrust, the defense is as follows:

• *Starting Position*: Basic defensive stance with your side to the attacker.

• *Action*: As soon as the knife thrust begins (191), step back with the covered forearm held up to protect the head (192). As soon as possible, attempt to put as much space between you and the knife as is necessary for your safety. If possible, redirect or parry the hand holding the knife (193). Immediately retaliate with a side kick to the shin or knee while you escape. Also, be careful to keep a safe distance from the knife by using the kick. If the assailant grabs onto you and thrusts with the knife, quickly pivot or turn away and immediately attack his eyes or groin. There will not be time to step back.

191. OVERHEAD KNIFE ATTACK—HOLD

192. OVERHEAD KNIFE ATTACK—STEP BACK

193. SLASHING KNIFE ATTACK—PARRY

- *Note*: Use any available object to help keep the knife away. Strike or block with a chair, table, piece of wood, or throw dirt into the eyes of the attacker. If by chance the attacker drops the knife, do not attempt to use it. Either retain it while you escape or throw it far away.
- *Practice*: Must be with a partner. Use a rubber knife, a sturdy, rolled-up piece of paper, or a small cardboard tube to practice. Thrust from both an overhead and sideward direction. Start slowly and increase to a more realistic speed.

Pistol

As a general rule, if a pistol is aimed at you, do nothing! Remain calm and very slowly try to talk to the assailant. Ask what he wants and comply with his every wish since death may be a very strong possibility. Any slight movement could cause the attacker to fire his weapon. Do *not* yell for help.

If a "pro" aims a pistol at a victim, the weapon will rarely be against his victim's body or within her arm's reach. He will place the pistol back near his hip and stay away from the reach of the victim. If robbery is the motive and the victim cooperates, the professional probably will not shoot his victim. He knows that the police typically search harder for a murderer than for a robber. On the other hand, the amateur with a pistol will probably be nervous and as likely to shoot as not.

The following defense techniques are presented to give a woman at least a chance to save her life, when death seems very likely. The pistol is drawn in the front of the body within arm's reach:

- *Starting Position*: Basic defensive stance.
- *Action*: Calmly start talking and raise your hands up even if not instructed to do so. This is a natural reaction

and should not surprise the assailant. Try to look at the assailant and not at the pistol. Keep your elbows low and try to raise one hand slightly higher than the other to catch the attacker's eye to the opposite side of the intended block (194). Immediately, twist the body out of the line of fire and strike the attacker's wrist or pistol with the other hand or forearm (195). Grab onto the pistol barrel being careful not to cover the muzzle.

194. FRONT PISTOL ATTACK—RAISE HANDS

**195. FRONT PISTOL ATTACK—BLOCK PISTOL BY
AND TURN BODY**

196. FRONT PISTOL ATTACK—GRAB PISTOL

Maintain control of the pistol and try to twist it toward the attacker's body. Use both hands (196). Try to get possession of the pistol. Yell for help if someone is near and retaliate with attacks to the eyes, throat, knee, groin, etc., while you escape. Do not attempt to use the pistol. Take it with you or throw it away. *Note*: The most important part of this defensive action is to move out of the line of fire of the weapon.

• *Practice*: Must be with a partner. Use a toy gun. Practice the hand raise and body turn. Timing is very important. This is the type of technique that must be practiced until it is perfect.

• *Note*: If a pistol is held at your back, the same type of defense may be used. Be sure to first establish the fact that it is a pistol in your back, not a finger or some other object. Start talking while slowly raising your hands. Turn your head to look over your shoulder (197). Say something such as, "What is this, a joke?" or "Come

197. **REAR PISTOL ATTACK—LOOK AND RAISE HANDS**

198. REAR PISTOL ATTACK—TURN AND BLOCK PISTOL BY

on—is that you, John?" Then initiate your defense. Twist the body around and out of the line of fire (198). Your wrist or forearm will also help push the pistol away from the back. Immediately grab the pistol and try to twist it back toward the assailant and out of his hand (199). Again, do not attempt to use the pistol!

199. **REAR PISTOL ATTACK—GRAB PISTOL**

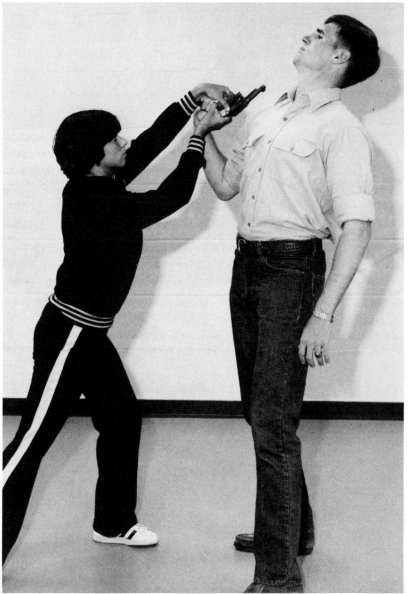

10 Rape Defense

Hopefully, the safety measures and self-defense techniques discussed in previous chapters are sufficient to prevent a rape from actually occurring. Rape, however, is a firm reality of our society. Number-wise, it is the fastest growing violent crime in the United States. The statistics regarding rapes are startling, especially with the consideration that at least half the rapes that are alleged to occur are not reported.

Rape is a crime in which a woman is forced to perform a sex act without giving her consent. It is a crime of violence, not sex. It is often performed to degrade, dehumanize and brutalize the woman. Women who have been rape victims often suffer emotionally for months and even years *after* the actual attack.

There are many myths associated with the crime of rape:

1. That rape victims provoke their attackers by acting or dressing seductively. This is pure

218

fabrication. A rape victim may be any age, may be very unattractive, and may be dressed in almost anything. What is important to the rapist is that the female victim be available and vulnerable;

2. That the victim enjoys and actually wants to be raped. On the contrary, most rape victims abhor the violence of the rape attack, and are in constant fear for their lives throughout the act;

3. That the woman could have resisted the rapist more forcefully. Most victims resist the rapist as much as is physically possible. In fact, police reports indicate that some women who were severely beaten following the rape probably resisted more than they should have;

4. That a rapist is a real "stud" and "he-man." This is untrue, the typical rapist is insecure about his masculinity; and,

5. That all men are potential rapists. On the contrary, a normal, healthy male seeks sexual gratification from a woman, while a rapist seeks something entirely different.

Whether or not to resist a rape attempt is an individual question. Every woman should decide if and how she should resist a rapist. It must be remembered that with rape the possibility of severe, even fatal, bodily harm exists. More and more rapists are murdering their victims to eliminate witnesses. One woman may decide that her life is the most important thing to her and cooperate with the rapist. Another may feel that the trauma of being raped would be so severe that she would rather take her chances and resist.

There are several verbal and physical techniques that may be used to defend against rape. There is no one *best* method to resist rape. Each individual must decide which technique is best for her. The following are some examples of how to defend against rape:

1. Do not panic. Remain calm and try to talk the rapist out of the assault. Many women have been successful in talking their way out of a rape attack. Tell him that you are pregnant, that you have VD, cancer or some other terminal illness. Try to get the sympathy of the rapist. In addition, if the victim appears to be relaxed, the rapist may decide that violence is not necessary.

2. Delay and stall for time. The victim may tell the rapist that she is ill and make herself vomit, or that she must go to the bathroom first. Complain of menstrual cramps, such men are often ambivalent about this condition. Suggest having either a drink or a meal first. Suggest going to someplace more comfortable. Never go to his place or yours. Any of these techniques may give you some time to better plan out what you are going to do, and may even cause the rapist to change his mind about the sexual assault.

3. If the rapist has a weapon, such as a knife or a pistol, it is probably best to do as he says. The victim's life is in danger and resisting would more than likely be futile. If by chance the weapon is put aside, then resistance again becomes a possibility. However, be careful.

4. If the victim decides to resist and there is a possibility that help is near, yell "Fire" to attract attention. Do not yell out if in a completely deserted area because the rapist might

be frightened enough by the noise to attempt to silence the victim forcefully.

5. If the victim feels that her life is in danger, and that she will resist no matter what, she should act quickly and viciously. Commit yourself completely to your own self-defense. Attack the most vulnerable areas of the assailant—the eyes, throat, nose, groin and knees. Show no mercy! Attack forcefully and be prepared to escape as soon as the rapist is momentarily injured, stunned or distracted. If possible, severely hurt and disable the attacker, do not just anger him. A woman is likely to have the advantage of the element of surprise since the rapist will not expect the victim to take up the attack herself.

6. The victim may pretend to cooperate, and when the rapist is peroccupied, and his guard is down, attack violently.

7. As soon as the victim is thrown to the ground, or the floor, the ground defense should be assumed and the defenses begun. This may prevent the rape assault from proceeding further.

8. The victim should not remove her own clothing, make the rapist do this. His hands will be momentarily occupied, which will make him more vulnerable to attack. The rapist is also vulnerable when he removes his own clothing.

9. Situation: The potential rapist is sitting on the victim undressing her.

- *Action*: Gouge the eyes (200), quickly get your feet under your hips and lift up, simultaneously throwing one leg over to one side. Push the rapist at the shoulders in the same direction (201). Follow up with an attack to the groin

200. **DEFENSE AGAINST RAPE—ATTACK EYES**

(202), stand up as soon as possible and escape. Be sure that the eye attack is severe enough to allow time for the release.

If the victim is raped, there are several things that must then be done:

1. Report the crime to the police immediately. Do not wait one hour or until the next day. Reporting the rape is essential and may prevent the

201. **DEFENSE AGAINST RAPE—HIP UP AND LEG OVER**

202. **DEFENSE AGAINST RAPE—AS ESCAPING, ATTACK GROIN**

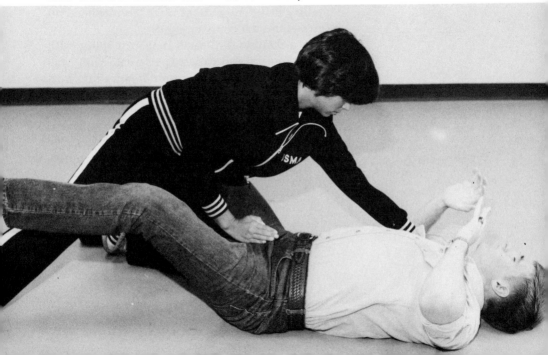

rapist from assaulting someone else. Too many rapes go unreported because of the fear and embarrassment of the victim.

2. Do not wash or douche yourself or, change, wash, or destroy any clothing worn at the time of the attack. This is all very valuable evidence.

3. Get medical attention immediately. This should include both a medical and an internal examination. This is for the victim's own protection as well as evidence of the crime. The victim may have been injured or given a disease (VD), or may even be pregnant as a result of the rape. Point out bruises, scratches, or any other injuries to the body. These may be photographed and used as evidence of the crime later in court.

4. As soon as able, the victim should inform the police of all the details of the rape attack—no matter how intimate. The victim should also try to give as complete a description of the assailant as possible: height, weight, age, color of hair and eyes, clothing; automobile if used, weapon if used, and anything else unusual that might help to identify the rapist.

5. The victim should be prepared to discuss the details of the rape later with the police, an attorney, or at a court proceeding.

6. Often a woman will need help in coping with the trauma of the rape experience. This help must start at home with an understanding husband, boyfriend, children, friend or relative. In addition, outside professional help may also be required. This is not unusual. In fact, in most instances, the rape victim should seek out professional counseling and advice. Individuals

who have training to assist rape victims include chaplains, priests and rabbis, mental hygienists, psychologists, and counselors. Several of the major cities, such as New York City, have Rape Crisis Centers, which offer valuable assistance to the rape victims.

11 Situational Defenses:

CITY AND COUNTRY

Several safety precautions and preventive measures exist that women should take in certain situations. Unfortunately, crimes and assaults involving women occur anywhere, at any time. Women should avoid potential dangers no matter where they may arise and should at all times be alert to their surroundings.

However, specific locations exist, both in the city and the country, where a woman could easily be attacked, and they require specific safeguards and actions. These localities include the following: (1) In the city: *public places*—a restaurant or bar; a motel or hotel; an elevator; and a theater; *public transportation* —bus; train; subway; and taxi. (2) In the country: a beach or park area; an isolated roadway, etc.

If a woman fails to heed the safety precautions and preventive measures presented in this chapter, and an assault on her is attempted, the self-defense techniques discussed in previous chapters will be required. A woman should never be embarrassed about defending herself in a public place. Attract as much attention and

assistance as possible, and do whatever else may be
necessary to protect yourself.

The City

More and more women frequent public places or are
using public transportation, either alone or with another female. Several precautions should be followed
for basic safety reasons:

RESTAURANT OR BAR

1. Go to reputable, well-populated, known res-
   taurants and bars. If alone, avoid an "out-of-
   the-way" place, even if the food is supposed
   to be "outstanding."
2. Avoid "swinging singles" places when alone.
3. Avoid sitting in dark corners. Try to face the
   entranceway and have most of the room in
   full view.
4. If alone, sit near the cashier, at the counter or
   at the bar, where assistance is available if
   needed.
5. Dress appropriately.
6. Generally, do not flirt with strangers.
7. If at night, be sure to park your vehicle close
   to the restaurant or bar, or take public transportation that stops directly at the front door.
8. Do not accept an offer from a stranger to be
   walked to your car or escorted home. Also, do
   not accompany an individual with whom you
   recently became acquainted to his home.
9. Notice if anyone follows you as you leave. If
   suspicious of someone, immediately return to
   the establishment and inform the manager.
10. If alone, do not accept food or drinks from a
    stranger.

11. If annoyed by someone verbally or physically, leave him and tell the manager. At times, speaking out in a loud voice, "leave me alone" will be enough to get rid of the annoyance. Do not be afraid of "making a scene."

12. If alone, be careful of how much personal information you give out to a stranger. Even if you meet an interesting individual and desire to meet him again, your first name only and a phone number should be sufficient information. He will call if he is genuinely interested.

13. Every woman should know her liquor capacity and not exceed it if alone in public. Alcohol dulls the senses and limits the ability to protect oneself!

MOTEL OR HOTEL

1. If alone, stay at a well-known and reputable motel or hotel, even if it is slightly more expensive or a little out of your way.

2. Be sure all windows and doors in the room are well secured. The door to the room should have a door chain and more than one lock.

3. Check to see if a switchboard clerk or desk clerk is on duty all night. This may be someone you can reach in case of an emergency.

4. Register using your last name and only initial of first name. This will help to prevent anyone from knowing you are a woman staying alone.

5. Leave valuables in the motel or hotel safe if one is available. If your valuables must be left in the room, hide and secure them as much as possible.

6. If you are alone, do not invite strangers into your room.
7. Answer the door to your room with caution, use the door chain or peephole to see who is at the door (this includes someone who is supposed to be room service or the maid).
8. When leaving your room, even for a short time, leave a radio or television on to discourage intruders while you are gone.
9. Be careful not to be followed by someone when returning to your room.
10. Have your key out unobtrusively and ready to open the door. Do not stand in the hallway searching through your purse for a room key.

ELEVATOR

1. Do not enter if a suspicious-looking person is in the elevator. Wait for the next car.
2. Before entering the elevator, check to be sure in which direction it is going. Do not spend extra time on the elevator riding in the wrong direction.
3. Upon entering the elevator, try to stand near the control panel. Push the alarm button to get assistance if necessary. If someone suspicious gets on, the buttons for several different floors may also be pushed so that the door opens frequently.
4. Another reason for standing near the control panel on the elevator would be to prevent someone else from turning out the lights or using the emergency stop. Women have been raped on elevators that had been stopped between floors.
5. Do not exit from the elevator if a suspicious-looking person is lingering in the hallway.

6. Be careful when exiting so that no suspicious individuals follow you, especially if you are alone. When in doubt, return to or stay on the elevator and ride to another floor. If you are still followed, go to the main lobby.

THEATER

1. If at night, be sure to park your vehicle close to the theater in a well-lighted parking lot. If taking public transportation, get off as close to the entrance of the theater as possible.
2. If alone, sit in an aisle seat or close to a family.
3. Keep your purse and any other valuables on your lap, not on the next seat.
4. Avoid sitting alone in either dark corners or in the balcony.
5. If annoyed by a stranger, immediately leave and tell the manager or an usher. Do not talk to the individual or show any interest at all.
6. Avoid going to theaters alone in unsavory neighborhoods—even if the most popular show in town is playing.
7. When leaving a theater alone, check to see that no one is following. If being followed, immediately return to the theater and get help.

PUBLIC TRANSPORTATION: BUS, TRAIN, SUBWAY, OR TAXI

1. Try not to travel alone, especially at night.
2. Know the time schedules for the different modes of public transportation. This should help you avoid a long wait for transportation.
3. If waiting for transportation, stand in a well-populated and well-lighted area. Avoid deserted stations and subway platforms. If very

few people are around, see if you can stand by a manned refreshment stand or change booth.

4. Always have the proper change ready when the transportation arrives. Do not display more money than is absolutely necessary. Use a separate change purse.

5. While waiting for transportation, be alert at all times. Never fall asleep in a bus or train station.

6. Sit near a driver, conductor or motorman. Try to find an aisle seat from which you can quickly exit if necessary.

7. Try to sit in a car on a train or subway with other passengers. If almost everyone exits, move to another car that has more people, or to a position next to the driver.

8. Always carry the proper change to make a phone call in the event you become stranded.

9. Hold your purse and packages. Do not put them on the seat next to you.

10. If annoyed verbally or physically, leave immediately and tell someone. Do not talk to the harassing individual or individuals involved.

11. If traveling alone at night, try to arrange to be met by someone at your point of exit.

12. While exiting a vehicle, check to see if someone is following you. If being followed, return to the vehicle. If possible, contact someone. If your vehicle has already departed, seek assistance at a residence or a place of business. Do not lead the potential assailant to your home.

13. If riding in a taxi, check to see that the picture

of the operator matches the driver. Also note the driver's name and identification number.

14. Taxi drivers are generally trustworthy. When requested, a driver will usually wait until a woman passenger is safely inside her building.

The Country

Many recreational-type areas are located in the countryside where a woman, alone or with other women, should be particularly careful. The following are preventive measures that should be taken:

BEACH OR PARK
1. If alone, try to avoid isolated or deserted beaches and recreational parks.
2. Generally, avoid "nude" beaches.
3. On a public beach, dress in appropriate swimming attire. Do not bathe topless or bottomless!
4. Do not leave valuables unattended while swimming or boating. It is wise to lock valuables in your car, and even better to leave them at home.
5. If annoyed by a stranger, leave immediately and inform someone of your difficulty, such as a lifeguard or park attendant.
6. If you are assaulted on a beach, several self-defense actions may be taken even if you are dressed only in a bathing suit and are barefoot: yell if assistance is near; throw sand in the eyes of your assailant; knee the groin; attack the eyes, nose and throat; stomp the instep with the heel of your foot; or side snap kick the attacker's knee or shin with the heel of your foot.

ISOLATED ROADWAYS

1. If driving alone, especially at night, try to avoid using deserted or infrequently traveled roadways.
2. Try to avoid roads that do not have periodic service stops.
3. If you must drive on an isolated roadway, be sure that your car is in excellent mechanical condition. Also carry emergency-type equipment: an extra gas can, flares, water, blanket, flashlight, and canned food.
4. If you have car trouble, put up the hood of the car, turn on your flasher, lock the doors of your car, and wait inside. Only walk for help if a service station or place of business is within sight. Be sure to walk facing traffic.
5. If lost on an unfamiliar road, and a stranger stops and offers to lead the way, do not follow. Remain in the locked vehicle and ask for directions.
6. Never pick up hitchhikers on an isolated roadway. Also, if someone is on the side of the road with car trouble, do not stop if you are alone. Drive to the nearest phone and call the police, or the AAA, or a garage to report the situation.
7. And while it hasn't anything to do with driving, if you're a walker or a jogger, do not use isolated roads if you're alone.

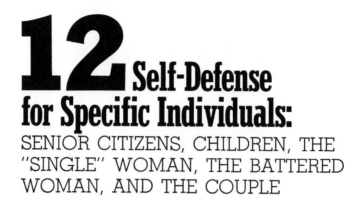

12 Self-Defense for Specific Individuals:
SENIOR CITIZENS, CHILDREN, THE "SINGLE" WOMAN, THE BATTERED WOMAN, AND THE COUPLE

In some self-defense situations, there may be a few individuals who, for some specific reasons, require special attention. These are extremely vulnerable individuals who should take extra precautionary measures in order to defend themselves. These people include senior citizens, children, the "single woman," "battered women" and couples. Since this group of individuals accounts for an extraordinarily high percentage of the assaults committed against women, they should be even more concerned about their personal safety than the average woman.

The Senior Citizen

Unfortunately, a would-be rapist is interested in all women, young or old, by virtue of their sex alone, regardless of their ages or appearances. The senior citizen, especially in the big cities, is more and more fre-

234

quently becoming a large part of the crime statistics involving women. However, just because a woman is "on in years" does not mean that she is incapable of defending herself. On the contrary, many of the self-defense techniques presented in preceding chapters can well be used successfully by the senior citizen. In addition to the preventive measures discussed in Chapter 4, there are other safety precautions that the senior citizen *in particular* should follow:

1. Ensure that one's residence is secure, that multiple locks are on all doors and that all windows are locked.
2. Try to live in a safe neighborhood where the neighbors are relatively near. Know your neighbors. Work out a plan for helping one another in an emergency. There is usually safety in numbers.
3. When going out, try to go with a friend, or better yet with several friends. If at all possible, avoid performing errands alone—especially if you are walking at night.
4. Do not carry valuables or large amounts of money. When shopping, carry only what is necessary. Put your money in different areas, e.g., purse; pockets; shoe, etc.
5. Do not display money.
6. Do not establish a set routine to do daily errands. Vary the time and the place both for shopping and outings.
7. Beware of purse snatchers and pickpockets, carry a small, obscure purse that has zippers and several compartments. If possible, do not carry a purse at all. Put your valuables elsewhere. If an assailant demands your purse or

valuables, do not hesitate to give them to him. Your life is more important than your valuables! If an assailant approaches and indicates that he wants your purse, hand it to him or drop it before he grabs for it and knocks you down. Many senior citizens are injured in this type of purse-snatching.

8. If home alone, have a light or radio on in another part of the house to give the appearance that someone else is home.

9. When actually leaving the house even for a very brief errand, such as putting out the trash; getting the mail; or picking up the newspaper, lock the door. It only takes a second for an intruder to enter your home.

10. Have a dog as a pet. Your pet does not have to be a trained "killer" dog. In many instances, even a small dog's bark discourages a potential prowler or attacker.

11. When out in public, be alert. Periodically check to see if you are being followed. This is especially important when returning from the bank or social security office. If someone is following you, immediately go to a residence or place of business for assistance. Do not lead the individual to your home!

12. If your keys are lost or stolen, change the house locks as soon as you notice keys are gone.

13. Be concerned about personal safety at all times. Do not be careless. Have confidence in your ability to prevent a crime before it happens.

Children

One of the most distressing sex crime statistics is that which involves a child. This may include a wide range of acts, from indecent exposure, abnormal sex acts, to actual sexual intercourse. The effect upon the child is often deeply injurious both physically and mentally. The trauma of this type of attack may take years to overcome.

It is the responsibility of parents and adults to educate children so that the possibility of assaults against them can be decreased and hopefully eliminated altogether. Crimes involving children should be prevented before they occur. The following are specific preventive measures for children:

1. A child should not take money, food or other gifts from a stranger.
2. A child should not accept a ride from a stranger even if he claims that he was sent by the child's parents.
3. Be sure that a child knows his/her name, address and phone number. This is essential information if the child is lost or injured.
4. Teach a child to use the phone in an emergency. Have the phone numbers of the police, fire department, and place of the parent's business or employment next to the phone in a highly visible place. At the very least, be sure the child knows how to dial "O" for operator assistance.
5. Know where your child is going and with whom. Get to know the child's friends and

their parents. Encourage your child to bring his/her friends to your house.

6. A child should not be out at night alone, and should avoid playing near empty or isolated areas. A child should not cut through alleys, vacant lots, or take other shortcuts at night.

7. If alone, a child should not enter the home of a stranger or even a casual acquaintance. Many of the cases of child-molesting are perpetrated by someone the child knows.

8. A stranger or casual acquaintance should not be invited into the home of the child, if the child is alone.

9. A child should be taught not to allow anyone —friend or relative—to touch or caress intimate parts of the body. If this should happen, the child should report it to his/her parents immediately.

10. A child should be told that if someone indecently exposes himself to the child, this should be reported to the parents immediately.

11. Parents should select baby-sitters with care. Know the individual before leaving the child alone with anyone.

12. A child should learn the importance of being careful, but should *not* develop an intense fear of all strangers.

The "Single Woman"

In addition to the preventive measures presented in Chapter 4, there are other safety precautions a woman living alone (especially in a big city) should consider:

1. If alone, select an apartment or home very carefully. Ask these questions: Is the building secure? Is there a night watchman or guard? May anyone enter the building at anytime? Are the locks on all the doors and windows workable and strong? Is the elevator self-service? Is the laundry room, storage area or trash receptacle located in an area secure from nonauthorized admittance? Is a garage located in or near the building? Is the neighborhood safe? Is the residential area well populated, well lighted, and convenient for shopping purposes? All of these things should be considered before renting or purchasing a place of residence. You may not be able to satisfy yourself on every count but, where you cannot, be extra alert about the potential dangers to which you may be exposed.

2. Avoid ground-floor apartments. These are more accessible for burglars and "peeping toms."

3. Keep all shades and drapes closed. Never dress in front of a window.

4. Do not advertise the fact that you are a woman living alone. List the name on the mailbox and in the phone directory with the last name and only the initial of the first name.

5. Be very careful about letting strangers into your home—even the new neighbor down the hall who wants to discuss a mutual problem about leaky faucets.

6. Do not linger in the laundry room. Put your clothes in the washer or dryer and return to your apartment until they are done.

7. Avoid using public transportation if traveling alone at night. Ride with a friend or take a taxi whenever possible.

8. If alone at night, avoid "singles" places—although the temptation to visit such establishments may be great.

9. Meet new male acquaintances through friends, at work, at church, or at any other such traditional place of social interacting. For example, participation in sports and athletic activities is an excellent way to meet someone with similar interests.

10. Do not hitchhike or take a ride offered by a stranger—even if you are late to work!

11. If going out on a blind date or with a stranger, meet him at a friend's house or in a public place. Also try to arrange a double date where you know the other couple.

12. If dating someone for the first time, tell a friend where you are going and with whom.

13. If going to a party alone, know who is giving the party and the type of party it is supposed to be. If alcohol or drugs are to be used, and they are of no interest to you, avoid the party. If you plan to drink, know your capacity. By becoming intoxicated, a woman diminishes her capacity to protect herself.

14. Avoid parking in a "lover's lane" area or strolling in the moonlight in a park. These areas may be romantic but they also attract criminal-types and other potential assailants.

15. If a party or a date turns out badly, call a taxi and go home. Do not stay around and be a "good sport."

16. Do not walk or jog alone at night or very early in the morning, no matter how populated the area may be.

17. Just because a date takes you dining and dancing, you do not owe him any sexual favors. Be honest and firm about your convictions, and do not flirt with, or tease a man, unless you are interested in him sexually.

The "Battered Woman"

The problem of the "battered wife or woman"— a woman beaten or abused by her husband or boyfriend —is a national problem, which no longer should be regarded as merely a "domestic squabble." Although wife-beating is a violent crime, it is one of the least reported crimes. Numerous women are beaten repeatedly, some to the extent that they require medical attention, but still they often do nothing about it. Some women fear being beaten again. Perhaps a greater fear is that their taking action will result in a divorce and their having to support themselves and possibly their children. Consequently, the "battered woman" tells herself that it will never happen again, or that she provoked the beating in the first place.

There are a number of things a "battered wife or woman" should do to help herself:

1. A woman should never allow her husband or boyfriend to beat her more than once. Do *not* believe your husband if he claims that it was an accident and will never happen again. Statistics strongly indicate that it probably will occur again, and again, and again!

2. Encourage your husband or boyfriend to get professional assistance or therapy. Help him to understand that he has a very serious problem.

3. The woman should not blame herself for being beaten or feel guilty that perhaps she provoked it. However, if a husband or boyfriend is known to easily lose his temper, try to remain calm when he is yelling or is visibly upset. This may avoid a confrontation in the first place.

4. If the woman is afraid that her husband or boyfriend will hit her again, she should leave the house at once. Go to a neighbor, or to a shelter for "battered women." Seek counseling, legal action, or whatever else is necessary. Do not wait around for the next beating!

5. If a woman has been assaulted, she should call the police and file a complaint. This is especially true if children are involved. Do not wait until the next time to get assistance because the next time it happens, he may kill you or harm your children.

6. A woman should seek help if she is a "battered woman." There are many possibilities for her. She is not alone! Telephone "hot lines" have been established in several cities to provide advice. Shelters are being established to get the woman out of the home and away from the attacker. A woman need not incur an assault more than once or suffer in silence!

The Couple

Every couple should decide ahead of time what they will do if attacked. There are times when a husband is seriously injured because he refuses to let his wife give up her jewelry or other valuables to a robber. A couple needs to decide before going out for the evening what they would do in a robbery or assault attempt. Almost invariably, if the assailant has a weapon, it is best to give up your valuables. In a life-or-death situation, the wife should let her husband know that his safety is more important to her than her valuables or even sexual "honor," hard as that may be to accept. Although most assailants almost never attack a couple without using a weapon, if such an attack is made, the couple should work together using self-defense techniques to ward off the attacker.

13 Defense Against Two or More Assailants

Most assaults against women involve only one assailant. Statistics, however, indicate that there are a few
gang-type attacks on women. Also some professional
thieves work in pairs. Fortunately, they normally are
only seeking valuables and are not intent on harming
their victims. In some situations, however, a woman is
forced to defend herself against two or more assailants.
Although her chances for escape are fewer, she
should follow a number of defensive principles if she
is attacked in this fashion.

In the first place, a woman alone should never be
walking in a neighborhood where youth-type gangs
hang out. If approached by such a gang, she should
remain calm. In most instances, the group may try to
frighten her with intimidating catcalls or obscene lan-
guage, but will probably not attack. If possible, the
woman should ignore the comments and continue walking. If stopped, she should speak with the group. This
should be done calmly and rationally. She should not

244

show fear. As much as possible, she should demonstrate complete confidence.

If by chance a gang consisting of three or more does decide to attack her, she should—for safety reasons—cooperate with their demands. Defending against so many assailants is extremely dangerous and almost impossible. The woman can save her life by *not* resisting in this type of attack situation.

The following are defense techniques that can be used against two or more assailants:

1. If a weapon is used, try to cooperate with the demands of the attackers.
2. Try not to let one of the attackers get behind you. Move to keep both assailants in front of you.
3. Defend against only one assailant at a time. Do not get in the middle of the two attackers so that they can assault you simultaneously. Try to stand closer to one of the assailants to pressure him to attack first. Assume a defensive stance, deliver a quick side snap kick to the knee or shin of the one attacker, then immediately turn to the other and kick. Quickly escape.
4. If in a populated area and attacked simultaneously by two assailants, do as in the aforementioned and yell "Fire!".
5. With two assailants, do not try to look directly at both at the same time. This would cause one's head to be constantly turning. Observe both of them by using peripheral vision.
6. In a situation with two assailants, if one grabs you with a rear hug and the other approaches you from the front, deliver a front snap kick

to the knee, shin or groin of the attacker in front (203); and then quickly escape the rear hug (204). Do not try to defend against both attackers at the same time. Eliminate the one to the front of you first.

203. 2 AGAINST 1—ONE IN FRONT AND OTHER WITH REAR HUG— KICK FRONT PERSON 1ST

204. 2 AGAINST 1—ONE IN FRONT AND OTHER WITH REAR HUG—
ESCAPE HUG HOLD 2ND

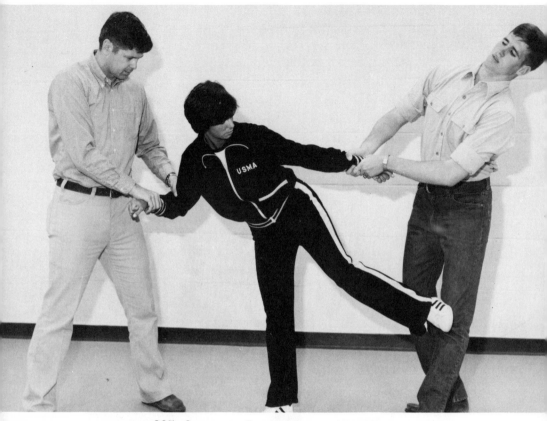

205. 2 AGAINST 1, BOTH HOLDING WRIST—
KICK ONE 1ST

7. In a situation where two assailants are each
holding one of your wrists, execute a single
wrist release first from one side (205) and
then from the other (206). Do not try to escape

206. 2 AGAINST 1, BOTH HOLDING WRIST—
KICK OTHER ONE 2ND

both at the same time. Try to escape the less
forceful hold first. Remember that a moving
and kicking victim is much more difficult to
assault.

8. If held by two assailants, with each holding one of your wrists and a third individual approaches you from the front and attempts to grab or strike you, defend against the oncoming assailant with a front snap kick (207). Follow with the wrist releases (Chapter 7) and several kicks while escaping as in number 7, above.

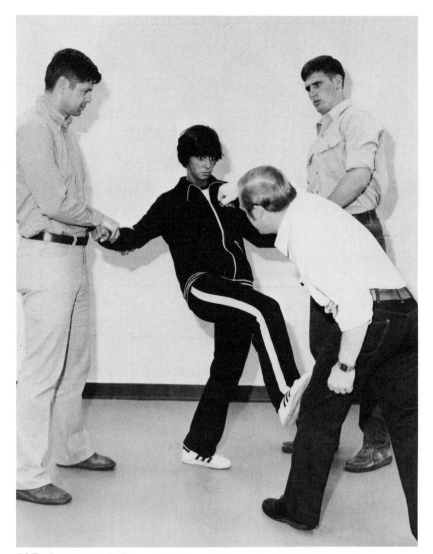

207. 3 AGAINST 1, 2 HOLDING WRISTS AND 1 IN FRONT ABOUT TO HIT—KICK TO FRONT PERSON 1ST

14 Recognizing Potential Assailants

Individuals who attack women have different characteristics and mannerisms. A woman should be able to quickly recognize the most common types of potential assailants. Not all potential attackers are seedy-looking middle-aged characters, who lurk on dark street corners. A young, attractive businessman-type, dressed in an expensive three-piece suit may also be a potential assailant.

The following are traits that should be recognized as common to some potential assailants:

1. A professional thief will most likely carry a weapon. His main interest is normally in the victim's valuables. If they are relinquished quickly enough, the victim will probably not be harmed. In addition, the "pro" knows the consequences of being caught and the severity of committing murder. However, be cooperative because he knows how to use his weapon and, if provoked, will.

2. The amateur thief with a weapon is much more dangerous. He is probably nervous and fearful. Any resistance on the part of the victim could trigger him to use his weapon. In many instances, he is under the effects of either drugs or alcohol. He probably is not rational. With this type of assailant, be very careful. Be calm and cooperative. Do not make any quick moves or gestures. Stay a safe distance from him if possible.

3. A "panhandler" or "street bum" typically wants any handout he can get. He probably does not carry a weapon. In most instances, he is harmless. In general, ignore this type of assailant and keep walking.

4. Potential assailants are not restricted to adult males. Women and teenagers may also be attackers. They should be treated just as seriously and with the same attacks to vulnerable areas—an exception here would be *not* to attack the female's groin area.

5. Be suspicious of strangers. However, in some instances, an individual who needs assistance may legitimately approach you. If it does not require you to subject yourself to personal danger, you should help him. If alone, it is probably best to refer him to someone or to somewhere else for help.

6. The common traits of a "typical rapist":
   a. The rapist is most typically eighteen years of age, usually under thirty. Generally, he is unmarried, unskilled, of low intelligence, has a low income, and is unsure of his masculinity.

b. Most rapes are planned. In at least half of the reported rape assaults, the assailant knows the victim. This may be a casual acquaintance, a date, a neighbor, a coworker, or a friend of a friend.

c. Most rapes occur in the warm months, on a Saturday, and between 8 PM and 2 AM.

d. Most rapes occur in the victim's own neighborhood, when she is alone and in an isolated surrounding.

e. Most rapes are not committed for sex but to degrade and dehumanize the woman. Many rapists have hateful and very aggressive feelings about women. Psychologists state that rapists want to "put women in their place."

f. In short, an individual often becomes a rape victim by being (for her) in the *wrong* place at the *wrong* time!

15 Self-Confidence:
THE KEY TO SURVIVAL

Preventive and precautionary measures, rape awareness information, and the most commonly needed self-defense skills and techniques have all been presented in *Self-Defense for Women: The West Point Way.* Any woman who has read this book now possesses sound information about personal safety. The next step is to actually apply the preventive measures and to learn the defensive skills. Preventive measures are easy enough. Defensive skills depend entirely upon the *individual.* Perhaps the ultimate question that must be answered by all women contemplating how they can and will act should they be assaulted is: Do I possess confidence in my ability to defend myself? In most such cases, self-confidence is the *key to survival.*

Building self-confidence is best accomplished through both mental and physical practice. Reading about self-defense techniques can be meaningless if these skills are not practiced and learned by the individual. Only through practice and application can a woman realize

254

that self-defense skills are not only attainable, but that they can work realistically in an attack situation. With confidence in her ability to protect herself, a woman will be well on her way to avoid becoming another statistic in our violent society.

Adequate self-defense for women is more than an exercise in wishful thinking. It should be the obligation of every woman—young and old alike!

ABOUT THE AUTHOR

Susan Peterson was the first woman physical education instructor in the history of the United States Military Academy. Currently, she is the Director of Women's Self-Defense and Special Adviser on Women's Physical Education for the Department of Physical Education, United States Military Academy, West Point.

Author of *An Improved Figure Through Exercise* and *The Complete Book of Tonus and Figure Exercise for Women*, Mrs. Peterson has appeared on several national radio and television shows, including the "Tonight Show" with Johnny Carson. Her self-defense background includes teaching in California, Illinois, and New York schools, presenting and attending numerous self-defense workshops and clinics throughout the United States, and working with the Military Police Branch of the United States Army, police departments in major United States cities, and martial arts experts. Her professional activities include serving as a clinician in the areas of self-defense and fitness exercise for the President's Council on Physical Fitness and Sport.